But I say unto you, Love your enemies, bless them that curse you, do good to them that hate you, and pray for them which despitefully use you, and persecute you;

-   MATTHEW 5:44

Every Christian must pass the test of absolute betrayal to go higher.

How will you answer when betrayal comes knocking on *your* door?

CAN YOU PASS

THE

Judas Test

by Glynda Lomax

The Judas Test

By Glynda Lomax

International Standard Book Number

ISBN-13: 978-1539050131

ISBN-10: 1539050130

Cover Design by Jason Alexander, www.ExpertSubjects.com

Scripture quotations from The Holy Bible, King James Version, unless otherwise noted, which is public domain in the United States.

A liturgical work.

Printed in the United States of America

And a man's foes shall be they of his own household.

- Matthew 10:36

Contents

Chapter 1 - Who Is Judas?

Few people walk through life without experiencing absolute betrayal at least once, and many will experience it numerous times. The Bible contains a number of stories about betrayal.

Most of us are familiar with the ultimate story of betrayal, the biblical story of Judas Iscariot. The story of the original Judas is found in Matthew 26, Mark 14, Luke 22 and John 18. Here it is.

JOHN 12:1-7

12 THEN JESUS SIX DAYS BEFORE THE PASSOVER CAME TO BETHANY, WHERE LAZARUS WAS, WHICH HAD BEEN DEAD, WHOM HE RAISED FROM THE DEAD.

2 THERE THEY MADE HIM A SUPPER; AND MARTHA SERVED: BUT LAZARUS WAS ONE OF THEM THAT SAT AT THE TABLE WITH HIM.

3 THEN TOOK MARY A POUND OF OINTMENT OF SPIKENARD, VERY COSTLY, AND ANOINTED THE FEET OF

JESUS, AND WIPED HIS FEET WITH HER HAIR: AND THE HOUSE WAS FILLED WITH THE ODOUR OF THE OINTMENT.

4 THEN SAITH ONE OF HIS DISCIPLES, JUDAS ISCARIOT, SIMON'S SON, WHICH SHOULD BETRAY HIM,

5 WHY WAS NOT THIS OINTMENT SOLD FOR THREE HUNDRED PENCE, AND GIVEN TO THE POOR?

6 THIS HE SAID, NOT THAT HE CARED FOR THE POOR; BUT BECAUSE HE WAS A THIEF, AND HAD THE BAG, AND BARE WHAT WAS PUT THEREIN.

7 THEN SAID JESUS, LET HER ALONE: AGAINST THE DAY OF MY BURYING HATH SHE KEPT THIS.

LUKE 7:36-39

36 AND ONE OF THE PHARISEES DESIRED HIM THAT HE WOULD EAT WITH HIM. AND HE WENT INTO THE PHARISEE'S HOUSE, AND SAT DOWN TO MEAT.

37 AND, BEHOLD, A WOMAN IN THE CITY, WHICH WAS A SINNER, WHEN SHE KNEW THAT JESUS SAT AT MEAT IN THE PHARISEE'S HOUSE, BROUGHT AN ALABASTER BOX OF OINTMENT,

38 AND STOOD AT HIS FEET BEHIND HIM WEEPING, AND BEGAN TO WASH HIS FEET WITH TEARS, AND DID WIPE THEM WITH THE HAIRS OF HER HEAD, AND KISSED HIS FEET, AND ANOINTED THEM WITH THE OINTMENT.

39 NOW WHEN THE PHARISEE WHICH HAD BIDDEN HIM SAW IT, HE SPAKE WITHIN HIMSELF, SAYING, THIS MAN, IF HE WERE A PROPHET, WOULD HAVE KNOWN WHO AND WHAT MANNER OF WOMAN THIS IS THAT TOUCHETH HIM: FOR SHE IS A SINNER.

MATTHEW 26:14-16

14 THEN ONE OF THE TWELVE, CALLED JUDAS ISCARIOT, WENT UNTO THE CHIEF PRIESTS,

15 AND SAID UNTO THEM, WHAT WILL YE GIVE ME, AND I WILL DELIVER HIM UNTO YOU? AND THEY COVENANTED WITH HIM FOR THIRTY PIECES OF SILVER.

16 AND FROM THAT TIME HE SOUGHT OPPORTUNITY TO BETRAY HIM.

MARK 14:3-11

3 AND BEING IN BETHANY IN THE HOUSE OF SIMON THE LEPER, AS HE SAT AT MEAT, THERE CAME A WOMAN HAVING AN ALABASTER BOX OF OINTMENT OF SPIKENARD VERY PRECIOUS; AND SHE BRAKE THE BOX, AND POURED IT ON HIS HEAD.

4 AND THERE WERE SOME THAT HAD INDIGNATION WITHIN THEMSELVES, AND SAID, WHY WAS THIS WASTE OF THE OINTMENT MADE?

5 FOR IT MIGHT HAVE BEEN SOLD FOR MORE THAN THREE HUNDRED PENCE, AND HAVE BEEN GIVEN TO THE POOR. AND THEY MURMURED AGAINST HER.

6 AND JESUS SAID, LET HER ALONE; WHY TROUBLE YE HER? SHE HATH WROUGHT A GOOD WORK ON ME.

7 FOR YE HAVE THE POOR WITH YOU ALWAYS, AND WHENSOEVER YE WILL YE MAY DO THEM GOOD: BUT ME YE HAVE NOT ALWAYS.

8 SHE HATH DONE WHAT SHE COULD: SHE IS COME AFOREHAND TO ANOINT MY BODY TO THE BURYING.

9 VERILY I SAY UNTO YOU, WHERESOEVER THIS GOSPEL SHALL BE PREACHED THROUGHOUT THE WHOLE WORLD,

THIS ALSO THAT SHE HATH DONE SHALL BE SPOKEN OF FOR A MEMORIAL OF HER.

10 AND JUDAS ISCARIOT, ONE OF THE TWELVE, WENT UNTO THE CHIEF PRIESTS, TO BETRAY HIM UNTO THEM.

11 AND WHEN THEY HEARD IT, THEY WERE GLAD, AND PROMISED TO GIVE HIM MONEY. AND HE SOUGHT HOW HE MIGHT CONVENIENTLY BETRAY HIM.

LUKE 8:1-2

8 AND IT CAME TO PASS AFTERWARD, THAT HE WENT THROUGHOUT EVERY CITY AND VILLAGE, PREACHING AND SHEWING THE GLAD TIDINGS OF THE KINGDOM OF GOD: AND THE TWELVE WERE WITH HIM,

2 AND CERTAIN WOMEN, WHICH HAD BEEN HEALED OF EVIL SPIRITS AND INFIRMITIES, MARY CALLED MAGDALENE, OUT OF WHOM WENT SEVEN DEVILS,

LUKE 22:2-6

2 AND THE CHIEF PRIESTS AND SCRIBES SOUGHT HOW THEY MIGHT KILL HIM; FOR THEY FEARED THE PEOPLE.

3 THEN ENTERED SATAN INTO JUDAS SURNAMED ISCARIOT, BEING OF THE NUMBER OF THE TWELVE.

4 AND HE WENT HIS WAY, AND COMMUNED WITH THE CHIEF PRIESTS AND CAPTAINS, HOW HE MIGHT BETRAY HIM UNTO THEM.

5 AND THEY WERE GLAD, AND COVENANTED TO GIVE HIM MONEY.

6 AND HE PROMISED, AND SOUGHT OPPORTUNITY TO BETRAY HIM UNTO THEM IN THE ABSENCE OF THE MULTITUDE.

Here is the same story, paraphrased:

One evening, Jesus was in Bethany, at the house of Simon the Leper, when Mary took an alabaster box of very expensive spikenard ointment, which she proceeded to anoint His feet with, wiping them with her hair.

The disciples, especially Judas, became indignant, saying the ointment could have been sold for a good deal of money, and that money given to the poor. The ointment was described as being worth 300 pence, possibly a year's wages in that time.

Jesus responded to their indignation by saying that she had done a good thing in anointing Him for His burial. He then added that wherever the gospel was preached throughout the world, it

> **Offense makes fertile ground for Satan to enter into any of us.**

would be told what she did, as a memorial of her.

Right after this incident, the Bible says Satan entered into Judas Iscariot and he went to the chief priests and asked them what they would pay him to deliver Jesus to them.

This was a golden opportunity for them, as they had just been discussing how they might get rid of Jesus, and they covenanted with him for thirty pieces of silver, and he promised them, and from that time, he looked for the opportunity to betray Jesus.

The Bible does not say a lot about Judas Iscariot, so we are left to imagine what his personality was like, what he was motivated by, what his goals and dreams might have been. It does, however, give us clues, so let's imagine that Judas was a little more carnal than the other disciples, since we have reason to believe he was by some of his actions, and imagine where his thoughts might have been in those final days before he betrayed our Lord.

Here was Judas, who probably believed that Jesus, who talked about His kingdom being established was going to become the next King of Israel, and that he was going to get the position of Royal Treasurer or some such thing. Just think of it! He would be known throughout history as the treasurer of a King! Surely Jesus, with His miracle-working power, could overthrow even Rome, and deliver everyone from their cruel power, so they would be heroes as well!

And now Jesus was talking about his burial? Clearly something was wrong!

What about your kingdom, Jesus? I thought we were going someplace big, that I was going to be your right hand man? And now you're saying this woman who just poured out a box of ointment worth a small fortune on you will be remembered for all time? What about me, Jesus? I've walked with you and done your bookkeeping, managed your money, and ministered with you these three long years. What about me? What do I get?

Judas almost certainly had become offended over the rebuke for questioning the woman's act of worship, which was when we are first told Satan entered him. Offense makes fertile ground for Satan to enter into any of us.

Judas so desperately wanting position and power in the present world, brings this verse to mind:

2 TIMOTHY 4:10 FOR DEMAS HATH FORSAKEN ME, HAVING LOVED THIS PRESENT WORLD...

It is possible Judas was attempting to force the hand of the Messiah, to show His true power and identity, to force Him to rebel against the Roman powers and thereby establish His Kingdom on earth.

We don't know for sure, but jealousy, resentment, frustration, and disillusionment may have been what motivated Judas to abandon the ministry of the gospel and betray Jesus.

Whatever the motives, it is clear that the evil desires in Judas' heart allowed Satan entrance and led him to create the biggest mistake in history, because Satan entered him and Judas set the plan in motion. Satan only comes to kill, steal and destroy, and he set about doing just that through the actions of Judas.

Sold out for thirty pieces of silver. In Exodus 21:32, it is the price of a dead slave. In Leviticus 27:2-7, it is the price of a live one. Jesus was sold for the price of a bond servant. Precious Jesus, the Son of God, the Prince of Peace, the King of Kings.

Satan will always attempt to land his most devastating blows on you by finding the weakest link in your intimate circle of loved ones.

Why did Judas sell his friend out so cheap?

Judas may have been less concerned about the money than the favor he would need with the chief priests when the ministry of Jesus collapsed. They hated Jesus, so they likely hated His disciples as well.

What was to stop them from rounding them all up and imprisoning or even killing them once they got Jesus out of the way? He knew how powerful they were, it could only be a matter of time until they found a way to get Jesus out of the picture. What would happen to him then? If Judas helped them now, perhaps they would remember his cooperation, perhaps they would show him favor then.

Or it could be that Judas had seen Jesus escape the authorities so many times that he actually thought He would get away again this time, and being none the wiser, leaving Judas thirty pieces of silver richer for it as he went on his way.

After Judas went to the Chief Priests and made the deal, he returned to Jesus and the disciples to celebrate the Passover with them.

Jesus told His disciples He was to be betrayed into the hands of men. Judas shook his head in disbelief when Jesus said this, acting as innocent of the coming betrayal as the others actually were, and perhaps curious whether Jesus really knew and would reveal the truth about him.

MATTHEW 17:22-23

22 AND WHILE THEY ABODE IN GALILEE, JESUS SAID UNTO THEM, THE SON OF MAN SHALL BE BETRAYED INTO THE HANDS OF MEN:

23 AND THEY SHALL KILL HIM, AND THE THIRD DAY HE SHALL BE RAISED AGAIN. AND THEY WERE EXCEEDING SORRY.

MATTHEW 26:25

25 THEN JUDAS, WHICH BETRAYED HIM, ANSWERED AND SAID, MASTER, IS IT I? HE SAID UNTO HIM, THOU HAST SAID.

Chapter 2 - The Many Faces of Betrayal

The dictionary defines betrayal as the act of delivering or exposing to an enemy by treachery or disloyalty; to be unfaithful in guarding, maintaining or fulfilling; to violate a confidence by revealing or disclosing in violation of confidence. True betrayal can only happen where there has been a closeness, an intimacy. And that former intimacy is exactly what makes absolute betrayal hurt so badly.

Judas knew Jesus' routines and the places He liked to retreat to and pray. He knew exactly where to find Jesus on the night he betrayed him. He knew because he had been one of Jesus' disciples, a privileged position of closeness and learning under Jesus' tutelage. The knowledge of Jesus' most intimate habits enabled Judas to betray Him easily.

Absolute betrayal is always committed by someone dear to your heart. Satan will always attempt to land his most devastating blows on you by finding the weakest link in your intimate circle of loved ones. Betrayal has many faces....the parent who abandoned you, the spouse who cheated, the friend who turned foe.....

LUKE 22:48 BUT JESUS SAID UNTO HIM, JUDAS, BETRAYEST THOU THE SON OF MAN WITH A KISS?

Notice in Luke 22:48 – Jesus basically asked Judas – are you betraying Me with a kiss? When the Judas Test comes, it will often be through someone kissing you and being affectionate to you one moment, and hurling accusations and turning you over to your enemies the next.

When the Judas Test shows up in our lives, and our reputation is threatened, our flesh reacts by wanting to defend and justify ourselves. We want to show we are in the right, were right about whatever we are accused of. We want to prove our position and shoot down our accuser's words. And often in a Judas Test situation, you actually *were* in the right, that's one of the things that makes it feel so bad - the accusations are unjust, or are at least mostly untrue, usually in a very unflattering or damaging way, and that's what makes it such a challenge to pass the test.

When the test shows up at your doorstep, you have the opportunity to prove whether you truly believe in crucifying your flesh and your own desires, or whether there's still enough of the old you left inside that you will try to vindicate yourself and justify your own position, and maybe even take vengeance against your accusers.

Let's take a look at what betrayal might have looked like in Biblical times.

Chapter 3 – The Original Betrayal – Satan – The Fall of the Prideful

GENESIS 3:1-6

3 NOW THE SERPENT WAS MORE SUBTIL THAN ANY BEAST OF THE FIELD WHICH THE LORD GOD HAD MADE. AND HE SAID UNTO THE WOMAN, YEA, HATH GOD SAID, YE SHALL NOT EAT OF EVERY TREE OF THE GARDEN?

2 AND THE WOMAN SAID UNTO THE SERPENT, WE MAY EAT OF THE FRUIT OF THE TREES OF THE GARDEN:

3 BUT OF THE FRUIT OF THE TREE WHICH IS IN THE MIDST OF THE GARDEN, GOD HATH SAID, YE SHALL NOT EAT OF IT, NEITHER SHALL YE TOUCH IT, LEST YE DIE.

4 AND THE SERPENT SAID UNTO THE WOMAN, YE SHALL NOT SURELY DIE:

5 FOR GOD DOTH KNOW THAT IN THE DAY YE EAT THEREOF, THEN YOUR EYES SHALL BE OPENED, AND YE SHALL BE AS GODS, KNOWING GOOD AND EVIL.

6 AND WHEN THE WOMAN SAW THAT THE TREE WAS GOOD FOR FOOD, AND THAT IT WAS PLEASANT TO THE EYES, AND A TREE TO BE DESIRED TO MAKE ONE WISE, SHE TOOK OF THE FRUIT THEREOF, AND DID EAT, AND GAVE ALSO UNTO HER HUSBAND WITH HER; AND HE DID EAT.

Satan, in the form of a serpent, showed up right after God created the world, the beautiful, lush Garden of Eden, and Adam and Eve.

Satan, believed to have been a beautifully created angel before the fall, betrayed God the Creator by tempting Adam and Eve to sin against Him, and destroy His original plan for them to live in abundance in the Garden. Satan was thrown out of Heaven because of pride. He wasn't content to be just beautiful, he wasn't content to live in all the beauty and perfection of heaven, he wanted *more*. He wanted what God *Himself* had. He doesn't hate God, he wants to *be* God.

There are many scriptures in the Bible that tell us what will happen to the prideful. Below is a sampling.

PROVERBS 11:2 WHEN PRIDE COMETH, THEN COMETH SHAME: BUT WITH THE LOWLY IS WISDOM.

PROVERBS 16:5 EVERY ONE THAT IS PROUD IN HEART IS AN ABOMINATION TO THE LORD: THOUGH HAND JOIN IN HAND, HE SHALL NOT BE UNPUNISHED.

PROVERBS 29:23 A MAN'S PRIDE SHALL BRING HIM LOW: BUT HONOUR SHALL UPHOLD THE HUMBLE IN SPIRIT.

PROVERBS 16:18 PRIDE GOETH BEFORE DESTRUCTION, AND AN HAUGHTY SPIRIT BEFORE A FALL.

PROVERBS 26:12 SEEST THOU A MAN WISE IN HIS OWN CONCEIT? THERE IS MORE HOPE OF A FOOL THAN OF HIM.

JAMES 4:6 BUT HE GIVETH MORE GRACE. WHEREFORE HE SAITH, GOD RESISTETH THE PROUD, BUT GIVETH GRACE UNTO THE HUMBLE.

JEREMIAH 9:23 THUS SAITH THE LORD, LET NOT THE WISE MAN GLORY IN HIS WISDOM, NEITHER LET THE MIGHTY MAN GLORY IN HIS MIGHT, LET NOT THE RICH MAN GLORY IN HIS RICHES:

PHILIPPIANS 2:3 LET NOTHING BE DONE THROUGH STRIFE OR VAINGLORY; BUT IN LOWLINESS OF MIND LET EACH ESTEEM OTHER BETTER THAN THEMSELVES.

Chapter 4 - Jealousy Over Your Acceptance By Someone and Their Lack of It - Cain and Abel

*E*arlier in the Bible, in Genesis 4, we find the story of Cain and Abel. Cain slew Abel out of pure jealousy.

GENESIS 4:1-7

1 AND ADAM KNEW EVE HIS WIFE; AND SHE CONCEIVED, AND BARE CAIN, AND SAID, I HAVE GOTTEN A MAN FROM THE LORD.

2 AND SHE AGAIN BARE HIS BROTHER ABEL. AND ABEL WAS A KEEPER OF SHEEP, BUT CAIN WAS A TILLER OF THE GROUND.

3 AND IN PROCESS OF TIME IT CAME TO PASS, THAT CAIN BROUGHT OF THE FRUIT OF THE GROUND AN OFFERING UNTO THE LORD.

4 AND ABEL, HE ALSO BROUGHT OF THE FIRSTLINGS OF HIS FLOCK AND OF THE FAT THEREOF. AND THE LORD HAD RESPECT UNTO ABEL AND TO HIS OFFERING:

5 BUT UNTO CAIN AND TO HIS OFFERING HE HAD NOT RESPECT. AND CAIN WAS VERY WROTH, AND HIS COUNTENANCE FELL.

6 AND THE LORD SAID UNTO CAIN, WHY ART THOU WROTH? AND WHY IS THY COUNTENANCE FALLEN?

7 IF THOU DOEST WELL, SHALT THOU NOT BE ACCEPTED? AND IF THOU DOEST NOT WELL, SIN LIETH AT THE DOOR. AND UNTO THEE SHALL BE HIS DESIRE, AND THOU SHALT RULE OVER HIM.

GENESIS 4:8

AND CAIN TALKED WITH ABEL HIS BROTHER: AND IT CAME TO PASS, WHEN THEY WERE IN THE FIELD, THAT CAIN ROSE UP AGAINST ABEL HIS BROTHER, AND SLEW HIM.

In vs. 8, it says And Cain talked with Abel his brother: and it came to pass, when they were in the field, that Cain rose up against Abel his brother, and slew him.

Abel's sacrifice had been more pleasing to God than Cain's was, and we can speculate, but we are not told for sure why. My friend Nicole taught me what I believe is the reason. Cain had ought in his heart towards Abel.

I believe Cain slew Abel out of jealousy. Abel's sacrifice was acceptable to God, Cain's wasn't. Cain became jealous and decided to eliminate the object of his jealousy, so he got him alone in a field, and while talking to him like nothing was wrong, he caught him off guard and murdered him.

MATTHEW 5:23-24

23 THEREFORE IF THOU BRING THY GIFT TO THE ALTAR, AND THERE REMEMBEREST THAT THY BROTHER HATH OUGHT AGAINST THEE;

24 LEAVE THERE THY GIFT BEFORE THE ALTAR, AND GO THY WAY; FIRST BE RECONCILED TO THY BROTHER, AND THEN COME AND OFFER THY GIFT.

Cain's sacrifice was not accepted because of the ugly thoughts in his heart about righteous Abel.

There are many reasons for betrayal. Jealousy is one. People who exhibit the traits of Judas tend to harbor a lot of jealousy.

Another story of jealousy and betrayal was King Saul's jealousy over the women's song about David.

Chapter 5 - The Popularity Contest - Jealousy Over A More Favorable Public Opinion - King Saul and David

Perhaps you are dealing with a betrayal by someone in your church or fellowship group. This is not an uncommon occurrence. It should be, among the people of God, but it isn't. Jealousy arises over popularity and promotion in the church the same as it does in other places. It happened to King David, it can certainly happen to us.

PSALM 55:14 WE TOOK SWEET COUNSEL TOGETHER, AND WALKED UNTO THE HOUSE OF GOD IN COMPANY.

King David would deal with betrayal again and again in his life. Whether because of the anointing, his earthly kingdom, his own sin, or other matters, betrayal showed up again and again.

In 1 Samuel 18, we see King Saul, chosen by God, who was previously David's friend, become jealous over David's reputation for military might with the people. The army was returning from battling the Philistines, and the women came out of all the cities of Israel, singing and dancing, to meet King Saul, but it was David they honored the most in their song, and from that day forward, King Saul looked for a chance to kill David.

1 Samuel 18:7-9

And the women answered one another as they played, and said, Saul hath slain his thousands, and David his ten thousands.

And Saul was very wroth, and the saying displeased him; and he said, They have ascribed unto David ten thousands, and to me they have ascribed but thousands: and what can he have more but the kingdom?

And Saul eyed David from that day and forward.

After Amnon raped Tamar and ruined all her prospects for marriage to a good man, her brother Absalom was furious. He set Amnon up to be killed behind David's back.

2 SAMUEL 13:22-37

22 AND ABSALOM SPAKE UNTO HIS BROTHER AMNON NEITHER GOOD NOR BAD: FOR ABSALOM HATED AMNON, BECAUSE HE HAD FORCED HIS SISTER TAMAR.

23 AND IT CAME TO PASS AFTER TWO FULL YEARS, THAT ABSALOM HAD SHEEPSHEARERS IN BAALHAZOR, WHICH IS BESIDE EPHRAIM: AND ABSALOM INVITED ALL THE KING'S SONS.

24 AND ABSALOM CAME TO THE KING, AND SAID, BEHOLD NOW, THY SERVANT HATH SHEEPSHEARERS; LET THE KING, I BESEECH THEE, AND HIS SERVANTS GO WITH THY SERVANT.

25 AND THE KING SAID TO ABSALOM, NAY, MY SON, LET US NOT ALL NOW GO, LEST WE BE CHARGEABLE UNTO THEE. AND HE PRESSED HIM: HOWBEIT HE WOULD NOT GO, BUT BLESSED HIM.

26 THEN SAID ABSALOM, IF NOT, I PRAY THEE, LET MY BROTHER AMNON GO WITH US. AND THE KING SAID UNTO HIM, WHY SHOULD HE GO WITH THEE?

27 BUT ABSALOM PRESSED HIM, THAT HE LET AMNON AND ALL THE KING'S SONS GO WITH HIM.

28 NOW ABSALOM HAD COMMANDED HIS SERVANTS, SAYING, MARK YE NOW WHEN AMNON'S HEART IS MERRY WITH WINE, AND WHEN I SAY UNTO YOU, SMITE AMNON; THEN KILL HIM, FEAR NOT: HAVE NOT I COMMANDED YOU? BE COURAGEOUS, AND BE VALIANT.

29 AND THE SERVANTS OF ABSALOM DID UNTO AMNON AS ABSALOM HAD COMMANDED. THEN ALL THE KING'S SONS AROSE, AND EVERY MAN GAT HIM UP UPON HIS MULE, AND FLED.

30 AND IT CAME TO PASS, WHILE THEY WERE IN THE WAY, THAT TIDINGS CAME TO DAVID, SAYING, ABSALOM HATH SLAIN ALL THE KING'S SONS, AND THERE IS NOT ONE OF THEM LEFT.

31 THEN THE KING AROSE, AND TARE HIS GARMENTS, AND LAY ON THE EARTH; AND ALL HIS SERVANTS STOOD BY WITH THEIR CLOTHES RENT.

32 AND JONADAB, THE SON OF SHIMEAH DAVID'S BROTHER, ANSWERED AND SAID, LET NOT MY LORD SUPPOSE THAT THEY HAVE SLAIN ALL THE YOUNG MEN THE KING'S SONS; FOR AMNON ONLY IS DEAD: FOR BY THE APPOINTMENT OF ABSALOM THIS HATH BEEN DETERMINED FROM THE DAY THAT HE FORCED HIS SISTER TAMAR.

33 NOW THEREFORE LET NOT MY LORD THE KING TAKE THE THING TO HIS HEART, TO THINK THAT ALL THE KING'S SONS ARE DEAD: FOR AMNON ONLY IS DEAD.

34 BUT ABSALOM FLED. AND THE YOUNG MAN THAT KEPT THE WATCH LIFTED UP HIS EYES, AND LOOKED, AND, BEHOLD, THERE CAME MUCH PEOPLE BY THE WAY OF THE HILL SIDE BEHIND HIM.

35 AND JONADAB SAID UNTO THE KING, BEHOLD, THE KING'S SONS COME: AS THY SERVANT SAID, SO IT IS.

36 AND IT CAME TO PASS, AS SOON AS HE HAD MADE AN END OF SPEAKING, THAT, BEHOLD, THE KING'S SONS CAME, AND LIFTED UP THEIR VOICE AND WEPT: AND THE KING ALSO AND ALL HIS SERVANTS WEPT VERY SORE.

37 BUT ABSALOM FLED, AND WENT TO TALMAI, THE SON OF AMMIHUD, KING OF GESHUR. AND DAVID MOURNED FOR HIS SON EVERY DAY.

Then, to make the betrayal even worse, Absalom went after his father David's kingdom.

2 SAMUEL 15:12 AND ABSALOM SENT FOR AHITHOPHEL THE GILONITE, DAVID'S COUNSELLOR, FROM HIS CITY, EVEN FROM GILOH, WHILE HE OFFERED SACRIFICES. AND THE CONSPIRACY WAS STRONG; FOR THE PEOPLE INCREASED CONTINUALLY WITH ABSALOM.

This last betrayal led to the death of Absalom, which also involved the betrayal of King David by Joab, after King David had issued orders that Absalom was not to be killed.

> *2 SAMUEL 18:14 THEN SAID JOAB, I MAY NOT TARRY THUS WITH THEE. AND HE TOOK THREE DARTS IN HIS HAND, AND THRUST THEM THROUGH THE HEART OF ABSALOM, WHILE HE WAS YET ALIVE IN THE MIDST OF THE OAK.*

Chapter 6 - Betrayal Because They Want You – Amnon and Tamar

nother type of betrayal appears in the story of Amnon, who set his half-sister Tamar up so that he could take advantage of her in 2 Samuel 13.

Amnon, coached by his wicked friend Jonadab, pretended to be ill and requested that Tamar come and cook for him in his chambers to make him feel better. When she did, he raped her, destroying any chance she had to ever enter into a respectable marriage and destroying her reputation as a virtuous woman.

When Amnon raped Tamar, he did not take only her virginity, he raped her of her purpose in life, because after that, no righteous man would take her. He played on her sympathies, and then targeted her vulnerability to get what he wanted from her, casting her aside like yesterday's newspaper after he had fulfilled his lust..

2 SAMUEL 13:13-19

13 AND I, WHITHER SHALL I CAUSE MY SHAME TO GO? AND AS FOR THEE, THOU SHALT BE AS ONE OF THE FOOLS IN ISRAEL. NOW THEREFORE, I PRAY THEE, SPEAK UNTO THE KING; FOR HE WILL NOT WITHHOLD ME FROM THEE.

14 HOWBEIT HE WOULD NOT HEARKEN UNTO HER VOICE: BUT, BEING STRONGER THAN SHE, FORCED HER, AND LAY WITH HER.

15 THEN AMNON HATED HER EXCEEDINGLY; SO THAT THE HATRED WHEREWITH HE HATED HER WAS GREATER THAN THE LOVE WHEREWITH HE HAD LOVED HER. AND AMNON SAID UNTO HER, ARISE, BE GONE.

16 AND SHE SAID UNTO HIM, THERE IS NO CAUSE: THIS EVIL IN SENDING ME AWAY IS GREATER THAN THE OTHER THAT THOU DIDST UNTO ME. BUT HE WOULD NOT HEARKEN UNTO HER.

17 THEN HE CALLED HIS SERVANT THAT MINISTERED UNTO HIM, AND SAID, PUT NOW THIS WOMAN OUT FROM ME, AND BOLT THE DOOR AFTER HER.

18 AND SHE HAD A GARMENT OF DIVERS COLOURS UPON HER: FOR WITH SUCH ROBES WERE THE KING'S DAUGHTERS THAT WERE VIRGINS APPARELLED. THEN HIS SERVANT BROUGHT HER OUT, AND BOLTED THE DOOR AFTER HER.

19 AND TAMAR PUT ASHES ON HER HEAD, AND RENT HER GARMENT OF DIVERS COLOURS THAT WAS ON HER, AND LAID HER HAND ON HER HEAD, AND WENT ON CRYING.

Chapter 7 - They Want Something You Have - Naboth's Vineyard

Manipulating circumstances and events to support their lies is a common tactic in betrayal, and at no time is it worse than when you are dealing with a Jezebel spirit. The Jezebel spirit can attach to a man or woman, and it is equally vile and destructive in either.

1 KINGS 21:1-16

21 AND IT CAME TO PASS AFTER THESE THINGS, THAT NABOTH THE JEZREELITE HAD A VINEYARD, WHICH WAS IN JEZREEL, HARD BY THE PALACE OF AHAB KING OF SAMARIA.

2 AND AHAB SPAKE UNTO NABOTH, SAYING, GIVE ME THY VINEYARD, THAT I MAY HAVE IT FOR A GARDEN OF HERBS, BECAUSE IT IS NEAR UNTO MY HOUSE: AND I WILL GIVE THEE FOR IT A BETTER VINEYARD THAN IT; OR, IF IT SEEM GOOD TO THEE, I WILL GIVE THEE THE WORTH OF IT IN MONEY.

3 AND NABOTH SAID TO AHAB, THE LORD FORBID IT ME, THAT I SHOULD GIVE THE INHERITANCE OF MY FATHERS UNTO THEE.

4 AND AHAB CAME INTO HIS HOUSE HEAVY AND DISPLEASED BECAUSE OF THE WORD WHICH NABOTH THE JEZREELITE HAD SPOKEN TO HIM: FOR HE HAD SAID, I WILL NOT GIVE THEE THE INHERITANCE OF MY FATHERS. AND HE LAID HIM DOWN UPON HIS BED, AND TURNED AWAY HIS FACE, AND WOULD EAT NO BREAD.

5 BUT JEZEBEL HIS WIFE CAME TO HIM, AND SAID UNTO HIM, WHY IS THY SPIRIT SO SAD, THAT THOU EATEST NO BREAD?

6 AND HE SAID UNTO HER, BECAUSE I SPAKE UNTO NABOTH THE JEZREELITE, AND SAID UNTO HIM, GIVE ME THY VINEYARD FOR MONEY; OR ELSE, IF IT PLEASE THEE, I WILL GIVE THEE ANOTHER VINEYARD FOR IT: AND HE ANSWERED, I WILL NOT GIVE THEE MY VINEYARD.

7 AND JEZEBEL HIS WIFE SAID UNTO HIM, DOST THOU NOW GOVERN THE KINGDOM OF ISRAEL? ARISE, AND EAT BREAD, AND LET THINE HEART BE MERRY: I WILL GIVE THEE THE VINEYARD OF NABOTH THE JEZREELITE.

8 SO SHE WROTE LETTERS IN AHAB'S NAME, AND SEALED THEM WITH HIS SEAL, AND SENT THE LETTERS UNTO THE ELDERS AND TO THE NOBLES THAT WERE IN HIS CITY, DWELLING WITH NABOTH.

9 AND SHE WROTE IN THE LETTERS, SAYING, PROCLAIM A FAST, AND SET NABOTH ON HIGH AMONG THE PEOPLE:

10 AND SET TWO MEN, SONS OF BELIAL, BEFORE HIM, TO BEAR WITNESS AGAINST HIM, SAYING, THOU DIDST BLASPHEME GOD AND THE KING. AND THEN CARRY HIM OUT, AND STONE HIM, THAT HE MAY DIE.

11 AND THE MEN OF HIS CITY, EVEN THE ELDERS AND THE NOBLES WHO WERE THE INHABITANTS IN HIS CITY, DID AS JEZEBEL HAD SENT UNTO THEM, AND AS IT WAS WRITTEN IN THE LETTERS WHICH SHE HAD SENT UNTO THEM.

12 THEY PROCLAIMED A FAST, AND SET NABOTH ON HIGH AMONG THE PEOPLE.

13 AND THERE CAME IN TWO MEN, CHILDREN OF BELIAL, AND SAT BEFORE HIM: AND THE MEN OF BELIAL WITNESSED AGAINST HIM, EVEN AGAINST NABOTH, IN THE PRESENCE OF THE PEOPLE, SAYING, NABOTH DID BLASPHEME GOD AND THE KING. THEN THEY CARRIED HIM FORTH OUT OF THE CITY, AND STONED HIM WITH STONES, THAT HE DIED.

14 THEN THEY SENT TO JEZEBEL, SAYING, NABOTH IS STONED, AND IS DEAD.

__15 AND IT CAME TO PASS, WHEN JEZEBEL HEARD THAT NABOTH WAS STONED, AND WAS DEAD, THAT JEZEBEL SAID TO AHAB, ARISE, TAKE POSSESSION OF THE VINEYARD OF NABOTH THE JEZREELITE, WHICH HE REFUSED TO GIVE THEE FOR MONEY: FOR NABOTH IS NOT ALIVE, BUT DEAD.__

__16 AND IT CAME TO PASS, WHEN AHAB HEARD THAT NABOTH WAS DEAD, THAT AHAB ROSE UP TO GO DOWN TO THE VINEYARD OF NABOTH THE JEZREELITE, TO TAKE POSSESSION OF IT.__

In 1 Kings 21, Jezebel pulled a Judas tactic on Naboth to get his vineyard for King Ahab. Jezebel wrote letters to have Naboth falsely accused and stoned to death. She wanted him completely out of the way, but she used others to entice and murder him.

Character assassination is one of the main weapons used in Judas Test betrayals. They will bring the accusers to you to cast lying stones at you until your reputation is dead in the water, so they can have their way.

Chapter 8 - Betrayed Because Of Your Own Sin - Samson

The story of Delilah's betrayal of Samson in Judges 16 is a classic tale of betrayal. Delilah didn't even try to hide what she was doing, but overconfident Samson thought he could handle whatever the Philistines could bring on. As it turned out, he couldn't.

JUDGES 16:1-21

16 THEN WENT SAMSON TO GAZA, AND SAW THERE AN HARLOT, AND WENT IN UNTO HER.

2 AND IT WAS TOLD THE GAZITES, SAYING, SAMSON IS COME HITHER. AND THEY COMPASSED HIM IN, AND LAID WAIT FOR HIM ALL NIGHT IN THE GATE OF THE CITY, AND WERE QUIET ALL THE NIGHT, SAYING, IN THE MORNING, WHEN IT IS DAY, WE SHALL KILL HIM.

3 AND SAMSON LAY TILL MIDNIGHT, AND AROSE AT MIDNIGHT, AND TOOK THE DOORS OF THE GATE OF THE CITY, AND THE TWO POSTS, AND WENT AWAY WITH THEM,

BAR AND ALL, AND PUT THEM UPON HIS SHOULDERS, AND CARRIED THEM UP TO THE TOP OF AN HILL THAT IS BEFORE HEBRON.

4 AND IT CAME TO PASS AFTERWARD, THAT HE LOVED A WOMAN IN THE VALLEY OF SOREK, WHOSE NAME WAS DELILAH.

5 AND THE LORDS OF THE PHILISTINES CAME UP UNTO HER, AND SAID UNTO HER, ENTICE HIM, AND SEE WHEREIN HIS GREAT STRENGTH LIETH, AND BY WHAT MEANS WE MAY PREVAIL AGAINST HIM, THAT WE MAY BIND HIM TO AFFLICT HIM; AND WE WILL GIVE THEE EVERY ONE OF US ELEVEN HUNDRED PIECES OF SILVER.

6 AND DELILAH SAID TO SAMSON, TELL ME, I PRAY THEE, WHEREIN THY GREAT STRENGTH LIETH, AND WHEREWITH THOU MIGHTEST BE BOUND TO AFFLICT THEE.

7 AND SAMSON SAID UNTO HER, IF THEY BIND ME WITH SEVEN GREEN WITHS THAT WERE NEVER DRIED, THEN SHALL I BE WEAK, AND BE AS ANOTHER MAN.

8 THEN THE LORDS OF THE PHILISTINES BROUGHT UP TO HER SEVEN GREEN WITHS WHICH HAD NOT BEEN DRIED, AND SHE BOUND HIM WITH THEM.

9 NOW THERE WERE MEN LYING IN WAIT, ABIDING WITH HER IN THE CHAMBER. AND SHE SAID UNTO HIM, THE PHILISTINES BE UPON THEE, SAMSON. AND HE BRAKE THE WITHS, AS A THREAD OF TOW IS BROKEN WHEN IT TOUCHETH THE FIRE. SO HIS STRENGTH WAS NOT KNOWN.

10 AND DELILAH SAID UNTO SAMSON, BEHOLD, THOU HAST MOCKED ME, AND TOLD ME LIES: NOW TELL ME, I PRAY THEE, WHEREWITH THOU MIGHTEST BE BOUND.

11 AND HE SAID UNTO HER, IF THEY BIND ME FAST WITH NEW ROPES THAT NEVER WERE OCCUPIED, THEN SHALL I BE WEAK, AND BE AS ANOTHER MAN.

12 DELILAH THEREFORE TOOK NEW ROPES, AND BOUND HIM THEREWITH, AND SAID UNTO HIM, THE PHILISTINES BE UPON THEE, SAMSON. AND THERE WERE LIERS IN WAIT ABIDING IN THE CHAMBER. AND HE BRAKE THEM FROM OFF HIS ARMS LIKE A THREAD.

13 AND DELILAH SAID UNTO SAMSON, HITHERTO THOU HAST MOCKED ME, AND TOLD ME LIES: TELL ME WHEREWITH THOU MIGHTEST BE BOUND. AND HE SAID UNTO HER, IF THOU WEAVEST THE SEVEN LOCKS OF MY HEAD WITH THE WEB.

14 AND SHE FASTENED IT WITH THE PIN, AND SAID UNTO HIM, THE PHILISTINES BE UPON THEE, SAMSON. AND HE AWAKED OUT OF HIS SLEEP, AND WENT AWAY WITH THE PIN OF THE BEAM, AND WITH THE WEB.

15 AND SHE SAID UNTO HIM, HOW CANST THOU SAY, I LOVE THEE, WHEN THINE HEART IS NOT WITH ME? THOU HAST MOCKED ME THESE THREE TIMES, AND HAST NOT TOLD ME WHEREIN THY GREAT STRENGTH LIETH.

16 AND IT CAME TO PASS, WHEN SHE PRESSED HIM DAILY WITH HER WORDS, AND URGED HIM, SO THAT HIS SOUL WAS VEXED UNTO DEATH;

17 THAT HE TOLD HER ALL HIS HEART, AND SAID UNTO HER, THERE HATH NOT COME A RAZOR UPON MINE HEAD; FOR I HAVE BEEN A NAZARITE UNTO GOD FROM MY MOTHER'S WOMB: IF I BE SHAVEN, THEN MY STRENGTH WILL GO FROM ME, AND I SHALL BECOME WEAK, AND BE LIKE ANY OTHER MAN.

18 AND WHEN DELILAH SAW THAT HE HAD TOLD HER ALL HIS HEART, SHE SENT AND CALLED FOR THE LORDS OF THE PHILISTINES, SAYING, COME UP THIS ONCE, FOR HE HATH SHEWED ME ALL HIS HEART. THEN THE LORDS OF THE PHILISTINES CAME UP UNTO HER, AND BROUGHT MONEY IN THEIR HAND.

19 AND SHE MADE HIM SLEEP UPON HER KNEES; AND SHE CALLED FOR A MAN, AND SHE CAUSED HIM TO SHAVE OFF THE SEVEN LOCKS OF HIS HEAD; AND SHE BEGAN TO AFFLICT HIM, AND HIS STRENGTH WENT FROM HIM.

20 AND SHE SAID, THE PHILISTINES BE UPON THEE, SAMSON. AND HE AWOKE OUT OF HIS SLEEP, AND SAID, I WILL GO OUT AS AT OTHER TIMES BEFORE, AND SHAKE MYSELF. AND HE WIST NOT THAT THE LORD WAS DEPARTED FROM HIM.

21 BUT THE PHILISTINES TOOK HIM, AND PUT OUT HIS EYES, AND BROUGHT HIM DOWN TO GAZA, AND BOUND HIM WITH FETTERS OF BRASS; AND HE DID GRIND IN THE PRISON HOUSE.

Delilah's betrayal cost him everything. Delilah's motivation was money. She sold Samson out for so many pieces of silver, plain and simple.

The difference in this story of betrayal is that Samson set himself up for this one. He put himself outside of God's protection by going in to a woman in the enemy's camp. He was a Nazarite, dedicated to God from his birth, and he was going in to a woman in the enemy's camp. When he gave away the secret of his strength when the Lord had told him not to reveal it, he had his head shaved, and the Spirit of the Lord departed from him because he had broken his Nazarite vow to the Lord.

Samson awakened, and he was so caught up in being with the seductive Delilah that he didn't even realize the Lord's presence had left him. When he tried to fight off the enemy, he was quickly defeated since he no longer had supernatural strength.

Sometimes we get ourselves into situations where we become mesmerized by someone or something the enemy sends to get us out of God's will, and we fall in love with the enemy. This is what happened to Samson - he fell in love with the enemy, and it cost him everything - his vision, his reputation and his position. We must be careful to keep our eyes on Jesus at all times so we do not ourselves become sport for the enemy.

> Samson fell in love with the enemy, and it cost him everything – his vision, his reputation, and his position.

Sometimes people on your job will set you up, especially out of jealousy. They will get close to you and act like they are confiding in you to get you to confide in them so they have intimate information to damage your reputation with. This has happened to me on jobs before, years ago when I was very naive and very trusting. Jealousy over the favor God had given me on a job turned out to be too much for another woman, and she used exactly this tactic. But God was on my side and her slander fell flat, and I became wiser for the lesson. The weapon had been formed against me, but God caused it not to prosper, because I conducted myself with honor and integrity (Is. 54:17). I never trusted her again. Sometimes we are betrayed because someone close to us wants something we have, or they want access to the influence we have.

The Judas Test can take many different faces, as we can see by examining the infallible holy Word of God.

This test will test your pride, your ego, your vanity, and how much you value your reputation. Not only that, but a Judas Test often assaults every one of these areas at once. Anyone whose pride, ego, vanity or reputation are important to them will be in danger of falling at higher levels if the Lord should promote them.

The famous Azusa Street Revival that took place in the early 1900's suffered a terrible hit by a Judas type betrayal. Pastor William Seymour's secretary took off to another state, taking his newsletter and donor subscriber list with her. She continued to send out the paper and receive the donations, teamed up with another evangelical leader in the Portland area, and effectively starved out the Azusa Street movement, which shut down not long after.

These are just a few examples of betrayals of trust like Jesus encountered when Judas kissed Him while driving the proverbial dagger into his back. The results of a Judas encounter are devastating, and can be life-changing.

Many Christian men and women have related to me dating stories that became horror stories as people jealous of their anointing or angry at being rejected after a few dates, turned on them so viciously they destroyed entire ministries. Others, apparently set up for attack by the enemy of their souls, allowed someone they thought they could trust into their life, who then proceeded to fabricate "evidence" of deeds never done, later used to bring shame and reproach. These deeds do not go unpunished. God is always watching.

As we see in the case of Samson and Delilah, all betrayal is not God ordained to promote us, though God will bring good out of it for the Kingdom, but sometimes betrayal is God ordained, as we see in the case of Joseph.

Chapter 9 - God Ordained Betrayal - Joseph

The great patriarch Joseph was betrayed by his brothers, who despised him for his prophetic dreams that they would someday bow down to him (Gen. 37) and likely for the favor their father Isaac showed him as well, favor that normally fell on the first born male.

GENESIS 37:1-28

37 AND JACOB DWELT IN THE LAND WHEREIN HIS FATHER WAS A STRANGER, IN THE LAND OF CANAAN.

2 THESE ARE THE GENERATIONS OF JACOB. JOSEPH, BEING SEVENTEEN YEARS OLD, WAS FEEDING THE FLOCK WITH HIS BRETHREN; AND THE LAD WAS WITH THE SONS OF BILHAH, AND WITH THE SONS OF ZILPAH, HIS FATHER'S WIVES: AND JOSEPH BROUGHT UNTO HIS FATHER THEIR EVIL REPORT.

3 NOW ISRAEL LOVED JOSEPH MORE THAN ALL HIS CHILDREN, BECAUSE HE WAS THE SON OF HIS OLD AGE: AND HE MADE HIM A COAT OF MANY COLOURS.

4 AND WHEN HIS BRETHREN SAW THAT THEIR FATHER LOVED HIM MORE THAN ALL HIS BRETHREN, THEY HATED HIM, AND COULD NOT SPEAK PEACEABLY UNTO HIM.

5 AND JOSEPH DREAMED A DREAM, AND HE TOLD IT HIS BRETHREN: AND THEY HATED HIM YET THE MORE.

6 AND HE SAID UNTO THEM, HEAR, I PRAY YOU, THIS DREAM WHICH I HAVE DREAMED:

7 FOR, BEHOLD, WE WERE BINDING SHEAVES IN THE FIELD, AND, LO, MY SHEAF AROSE, AND ALSO STOOD UPRIGHT; AND, BEHOLD, YOUR SHEAVES STOOD ROUND ABOUT, AND MADE OBEISANCE TO MY SHEAF.

8 AND HIS BRETHREN SAID TO HIM, SHALT THOU INDEED REIGN OVER US? OR SHALT THOU INDEED HAVE DOMINION OVER US? AND THEY HATED HIM YET THE MORE FOR HIS DREAMS, AND FOR HIS WORDS.

9 AND HE DREAMED YET ANOTHER DREAM, AND TOLD IT HIS BRETHREN, AND SAID, BEHOLD, I HAVE DREAMED A DREAM MORE; AND, BEHOLD, THE SUN AND THE MOON AND THE ELEVEN STARS MADE OBEISANCE TO ME.

10 AND HE TOLD IT TO HIS FATHER, AND TO HIS BRETHREN: AND HIS FATHER REBUKED HIM, AND SAID UNTO HIM,

WHAT IS THIS DREAM THAT THOU HAST DREAMED? SHALL I AND THY MOTHER AND THY BRETHREN INDEED COME TO BOW DOWN OURSELVES TO THEE TO THE EARTH?

11 AND HIS BRETHREN ENVIED HIM; BUT HIS FATHER OBSERVED THE SAYING.

12 AND HIS BRETHREN WENT TO FEED THEIR FATHER'S FLOCK IN SHECHEM.

13 AND ISRAEL SAID UNTO JOSEPH, DO NOT THY BRETHREN FEED THE FLOCK IN SHECHEM? COME, AND I WILL SEND THEE UNTO THEM. AND HE SAID TO HIM, HERE AM I.

14 AND HE SAID TO HIM, GO, I PRAY THEE, SEE WHETHER IT BE WELL WITH THY BRETHREN, AND WELL WITH THE FLOCKS; AND BRING ME WORD AGAIN. SO HE SENT HIM OUT OF THE VALE OF HEBRON, AND HE CAME TO SHECHEM.

15 AND A CERTAIN MAN FOUND HIM, AND, BEHOLD, HE WAS WANDERING IN THE FIELD: AND THE MAN ASKED HIM, SAYING, WHAT SEEKEST THOU?

16 AND HE SAID, I SEEK MY BRETHREN: TELL ME, I PRAY THEE, WHERE THEY FEED THEIR FLOCKS.

17 AND THE MAN SAID, THEY ARE DEPARTED HENCE; FOR I HEARD THEM SAY, LET US GO TO DOTHAN. AND JOSEPH WENT AFTER HIS BRETHREN, AND FOUND THEM IN DOTHAN.

18 AND WHEN THEY SAW HIM AFAR OFF, EVEN BEFORE HE CAME NEAR UNTO THEM, THEY CONSPIRED AGAINST HIM TO SLAY HIM.

19 AND THEY SAID ONE TO ANOTHER, BEHOLD, THIS DREAMER COMETH.

20 COME NOW THEREFORE, AND LET US SLAY HIM, AND CAST HIM INTO SOME PIT, AND WE WILL SAY, SOME EVIL BEAST HATH DEVOURED HIM: AND WE SHALL SEE WHAT WILL BECOME OF HIS DREAMS.

21 AND REUBEN HEARD IT, AND HE DELIVERED HIM OUT OF THEIR HANDS; AND SAID, LET US NOT KILL HIM.

22 AND REUBEN SAID UNTO THEM, SHED NO BLOOD, BUT CAST HIM INTO THIS PIT THAT IS IN THE WILDERNESS, AND LAY NO HAND UPON HIM; THAT HE MIGHT RID HIM OUT OF THEIR HANDS, TO DELIVER HIM TO HIS FATHER AGAIN.

23 AND IT CAME TO PASS, WHEN JOSEPH WAS COME UNTO HIS BRETHREN, THAT THEY STRIPT JOSEPH OUT OF HIS COAT, HIS COAT OF MANY COLOURS THAT WAS ON HIM;

24 AND THEY TOOK HIM, AND CAST HIM INTO A PIT: AND THE PIT WAS EMPTY, THERE WAS NO WATER IN IT.

25 AND THEY SAT DOWN TO EAT BREAD: AND THEY LIFTED UP THEIR EYES AND LOOKED, AND, BEHOLD, A COMPANY OF ISHMEELITES CAME FROM GILEAD WITH THEIR CAMELS BEARING SPICERY AND BALM AND MYRRH, GOING TO CARRY IT DOWN TO EGYPT.

26 AND JUDAH SAID UNTO HIS BRETHREN, WHAT PROFIT IS IT IF WE SLAY OUR BROTHER, AND CONCEAL HIS BLOOD?

27 COME, AND LET US SELL HIM TO THE ISHMEELITES, AND LET NOT OUR HAND BE UPON HIM; FOR HE IS OUR BROTHER AND OUR FLESH. AND HIS BRETHREN WERE CONTENT.

28 THEN THERE PASSED BY MIDIANITES MERCHANTMEN; AND THEY DREW AND LIFTED UP JOSEPH OUT OF THE PIT, AND SOLD JOSEPH TO THE ISHMEELITES FOR TWENTY PIECES OF SILVER: AND THEY BROUGHT JOSEPH INTO EGYPT.

Some say Joseph was prideful in sharing his dreams, but in all the other scriptures, Joseph appears to be both wise and humble, and may have just been sharing everyday experiences with his brothers, a normal and natural thing to do. They, however, did not take it very well.

They actually conspired to kill him, but instead sold him to some passing merchants, who carried him away into Egypt.

Joseph was later also betrayed by Potiphar's wife, who tried to seduce him but was rejected. She was angry that Joseph would not comply with her request to lay with her, and so, using his robe he had dropped in his haste to escape her seductive set-up as false evidence, fabricates a tale that *he* was trying to seduce *her*, which was completely untrue, but she manipulated the evidence enough to make it appear possible.

> Judas tests often make a show of false evidence to convict the innocent in the court of public opinion...

I find it very interesting that Joseph's brothers betrayed him with his robe of many colors, which was a garment that marked him as his Father's favorite to inherit the firstborn's share, and Potiphar's wife betrayed him with his robe as well, by making it look as if he had left it after attempting to take advantage of her.

Judas tests often make a show of false evidence to convict the innocent in the court of public opinion, just as the chief priests tried to make Jesus look guilty of blasphemy. Beware of this tactic, saints!

Chapter 10 - Walking Through Betrayal

When a Judas Test comes, we need to remember that God allowed it to come. We may be misunderstood, or perhaps have associated ourselves with another ministry or minister that is criticized or falls from high opinion, and we are attacked because of that. We may be accused of things we did not do, or someone thinks we said something or spread some false doctrine because they misunderstood our message. How it comes is not important, but why it is there, is.

There are few experiences in life as painful as being betrayed by someone you love or care about. Not only do you lose the relationship as you knew it, but what you feel for them turns on you like a weapon. That is precisely why the enemy can devastate us so completely with betrayal.

While you reel from the shock, hurt and anger of how your spouse or child, best friend or other loved one turned on you and drove those daggers into your back, the enemy is also using them to cut into your ability to trust, to hope, to dream, and to minister to others.

Betrayal at this level changes something inside you forever.

Many years ago, a woman I worked with related to me how her husband had cheated on her with her long time best friend. She divorced him, dumped the "friend," and stopped trusting people altogether. Satan had destroyed her ability to trust, and to love again. She refused to even date.

> Everyone must pass the Judas Test before they can be promoted.

In recent years, I experienced the betrayal of a very close friend. A person I confided in, shared all I had with, helped every way I could. I later discovered my friend was not a friend at all, and had been not only speaking negatively behind my back to people I loved, but genuinely trying to hurt me with their actions, while spending time with me and acting like someone I could trust. When I discovered it, I stopped the relationship immediately.

Though I ended the relationship, the pain of being betrayed went on and on and on. This was someone I trusted! Someone I loved! Someone I helped financially. Someone I thought loved me back, but the enemy entered their dark heart just as he had filled the heart of Judas Iscariot so many years ago.

I searched my heart and my memory, and I knew without a doubt I had never done one thing against my friend. I knew my heart was both true and loyal and I did not deserve to be betrayed. The betrayal came at the worst possible time for me, needless to say, as it often does. Seeing the unjustified attack, I set myself to pass the test. God was testing me to see if I was ready for promotion. I determined I would not let my emotions make me fail the test and lose whatever promotion God wanted to give to me.

At the point when you hurt the most, it is important to remember to praise God for what is happening. We do this, because if it was allowed, He must have a purpose for it that will turn out to your benefit. That is the time when it is most difficult to praise, but it is a sign you trust the Lord with the whole situation and when you are deep in the heart of a serious betrayal, it is comforting to know you *can* trust God with what is happening.

Late one night near the end of 2011, I was praying for a friend who was suffering a terrible betrayal and slander campaign by a former close friend and ministry partner, when the Lord spoke this to me:

"Everyone must pass The Judas Test before they can be promoted. They must walk in love when they are betrayed as My Son Jesus did."

MATTHEW 24:10

AND THEN SHALL MANY BE OFFENDED, AND SHALL BETRAY ONE ANOTHER, AND SHALL HATE ONE ANOTHER.

LUKE 21:16

AND YE SHALL BE BETRAYED BOTH BY PARENTS, AND BRETHREN, AND KINSFOLKS, AND FRIENDS; AND SOME OF YOU SHALL THEY CAUSE TO BE PUT TO DEATH.

We live in perilous times. Betrayals will become both more frequent and more deadly to us as Christians, and we cannot change that, because scripture must be fulfilled. It is to our benefit to practice responding as Jesus did, not as the enemy would have us respond, and not as our flesh and emotions want to respond. If we do not, the pain of the many betrayals that are coming will cause our Christ-like love to grow cold, and we will become bitter shells of the caring Christians we are now.

The Lord asked me to write this book to tell His children about the Judas Test, its purpose, and what He wants us to do to pass it. He also said the reason is because in the future betrayals will be commonplace in our lives, and we will need to know more about it.

The Judas Test is the test of whether you can walk in love in the face of absolute betrayal by someone or more than one someone really close to you that you loved and trusted, someone who walked with you along your journey, someone whose life you have sown into. More often than not, someone you helped.

REALIZE YOUR ACCUSERS HAVE NO POWER OVER YOU BUT WHAT GOD HAS ALLOWED

JOHN 19:11

JESUS ANSWERED, THOU COULDEST HAVE NO POWER AT ALL AGAINST ME, EXCEPT IT WERE GIVEN THEE FROM ABOVE: THEREFORE HE THAT DELIVERED ME UNTO THEE HATH THE GREATER SIN.

JOHN 18:11 - SHALL I NOT DRINK THE CUP?

11 THEN SAID JESUS UNTO PETER, PUT UP THY SWORD INTO THE SHEATH: THE CUP WHICH MY FATHER HATH GIVEN ME, SHALL I NOT DRINK IT?

If you are experiencing betrayal, your goal as a Christian should be to pass through it responding as much like Jesus did and would as you can.

Fiery darts

Taking a direct hit through someone you've walked with and ministered to is far more painful than when a random stranger talks bad about or to you. It stirs up our emotions. That's one of the reasons it's so important to keep our emotions in check at all times.

Often our first emotion is denial. They would *never* do that, right? Then the proof appears before our eyes and we know that indeed they have. The shock comes next. Shock that this person we cared so deeply for and tried to help has turned on us, then grief over the loss of the relationship.

Often our first instinct is to answer the accusations, but that's not what Jesus did. It is far more important to look at the situation in terms of the long run. Is it really going to matter 5 years from now whether you answered or not?

PROVERBS 29:20

SEEST THOU A MAN THAT IS HASTY IN HIS WORDS? THERE IS MORE HOPE OF A FOOL THAN OF HIM.

PROVERBS 29:11

A FOOL UTTERETH ALL HIS MIND: BUT A WISE MAN KEEPETH IT IN TILL AFTERWARDS.

AND MY PERSONAL FAVORITE:

ECCLESIASTES 7:9

BE NOT HASTY IN THY SPIRIT TO BE ANGRY: FOR ANGER RESTETH IN THE BOSOM OF FOOLS.

Judas is hoping you *will* answer hastily and utter all your mind, because he knows he can turn every negative word you utter around and slander you further. Still want to answer that accusation? When strife knocks at our doors, we don't need to answer it.

And if we jump on the slander wagon, we are sowing seeds that can only come back as a harvest in our own lives. Talking bad about someone, even if you know they talked bad about you first, even if every word you say is the truth, never, ever brings a good result. Character assassination of your accuser is just murder in another form, the murder of their reputation, the murder of potential, and of friendships, and it demotes you to their level. We want to go *up*, not down. It will make you look like exactly what you are, an angry, hurt and vengeful person. Leave the paybacks to God.

Chapter 11 - Word Wounds - Destroy the Fiery Darts!

In 2009, I befriended a lady on the internet I really liked. We began emailing each other daily and talking on the phone often. She encouraged me to share with her and her husband any word the Lord gave me for them. Since I always pray for my friends, the Lord did end up giving me a message for them. When I relayed it, she completely rejected both God's message and me as well, and began insulting me. I felt the fiery darts land in my spirit and quickly ended the conversation. I felt like someone had fired something into my stomach. The Lord then told me to pull the fiery darts out and plead the Blood of Jesus over the wounds to heal them. I immediately obeyed and the pain stopped. I have used that method ever since. It will work for you, too.

ROMANS 12:19

DEARLY BELOVED, AVENGE NOT YOURSELVES, BUT RATHER GIVE PLACE UNTO WRATH: FOR IT IS WRITTEN, VENGEANCE IS MINE; I WILL REPAY, SAITH THE LORD.

If you get caught up in the strife and fighting, bitterness has a chance to root in your heart. Hate and anger may shield you from the pain temporarily, but eventually they will overwhelm you and harden your heart against everything that's good as well. Then unforgiveness will be there, something no Christian should have. Not after Jesus has forgiven us for so much.

We must trust God to deal with any vengeance that needs to be meted out. We must trust Him and be at peace regardless of whether He pays the person back and we know it or He doesn't, because that is truly His business and not ours. This is a bitter pill to swallow when you're really angry at the other party, or when you have suffered great loss, but once you truly forgive them and let go, it isn't so hard.

People who listen to slanderous accusations against you will believe what they choose to believe. True and loyal friends will stand with you when you stand accused, but if they don't, the Lord will be your strong tower. He will be your shield. He will prepare a table before you in the presence of your enemies. And He is well able to turn the entire situation to your benefit.

PSALM 61:3

FOR THOU HAST BEEN A SHELTER FOR ME, AND A STRONG TOWER FROM THE ENEMY.

PSALM 3:3

BUT THOU, O LORD, ART A SHIELD FOR ME; MY GLORY, AND THE LIFTER UP OF MINE HEAD.

Remember - you're up for promotion or you wouldn't be facing the Judas Test in the first place.

As the stories and lies and internet postings circulate, we feel shame and humiliation and we are helpless to change it. We must remember that Jesus made Himself of no reputation. We cannot hang our hats on what this world values, only on eternal things.

PHILIPPIANS 2:7

BUT MADE HIMSELF OF NO REPUTATION, AND TOOK UPON HIM THE FORM OF A SERVANT, AND WAS MADE IN THE LIKENESS OF MEN:

We feel sadness over the situation, the lost relationship, the ugly mess we are faced with. And we also feel anger. Anger at the injustice of it all. As our emotions make themselves known, we must fight hard against the desire to avenge ourselves, as vengeance is reserved for God alone.

We will sometimes fight the battle of jealousy as we see church members, friends or family members 'defect' and side with our accusers against us, believing the slanderous accusations. I think this is one of the most painful parts of this kind of betrayal, maybe because it adds to your loss in such a big way. At no time do you need all close to you as much as now.

Jesus wasn't the only one betrayed by Judas, the disciples all were as well. He was their life, following "The Way," as it was called then, was their life.

They had given up everything for The Way - their vocations, their daily routines. They had heard their wives and families and friends tell them they were crazy for following the carpenter from Nazareth around and listening to his stories.

They had laid down so much, and now one of their own - Judas! - had destroyed it all. How would Jesus' Kingdom ever come now? What would they do now - how could they ever go back to just being fishermen and tax collectors after all He had shown them, all He had taught them? They didn't have a contingency plan for if everything fell apart, because no matter what happened, Jesus had always had a solution. He could even quiet storms and feed thousands of people with almost nothing! No one else they knew could do that!

Chapter 12 - The Jesus Response

What Judas Iscariot did came as no surprise to Jesus. He knew what was coming, and that it was His life's purpose to submit to it. That's why He was praying so fervently in the Garden of Gethsemane the night before, when He was arrested.

Some say Iscariot means Dagger-Man, which comes from the Latin word *sicarius*. The Sicarii were a group of rebel assassins who resisted the Roman occupation of the country they lived in. So Judas already had rebellion in his blood.

Jesus knew before Passover that Judas was about to betray Him, but He also knew in His case it was part of the overall plan of the Cross, and He did not fight it. He loved Judas, but He did not try to show Judas all the scriptures that showed how wrong he was to betray Him, or threaten him with consequences when he did. He didn't remind him of how He'd sown into his life for three years as they walked and ministered together, how He had prayed for him and taught him mysteries no one else knew.

Jesus knew passing the Judas Test was part of God's overall plan.

It is unlikely that we will know ahead of time when we are about to be betrayed, but our singular focus needs to be to pass the test in Christ-like manner. This is the whole purpose of this book.

So let's talk about some ways we can pass the Judas Test walking through it in love. How did Jesus do it?

MATTHEW 27:12

12 AND WHEN HE WAS ACCUSED OF THE CHIEF PRIESTS AND ELDERS, HE ANSWERED NOTHING.

- Jesus answered not His accusers. We don't need to answer ours, either.

- Jesus interceded for those who accused and crucified Him, even as He was being crucified . We are instructed to pray for our enemies (that includes frenemies, too) and bless and do not curse them.

LUKE 23:34

34 THEN SAID JESUS, FATHER, FORGIVE THEM; FOR THEY KNOW NOT WHAT THEY DO. AND THEY PARTED HIS RAIMENT, AND CAST LOTS.

MATTHEW 5:44

44 BUT I SAY UNTO YOU, LOVE YOUR ENEMIES, BLESS THEM THAT
CURSE YOU, DO GOOD TO THEM THAT HATE YOU, AND PRAY FOR THEM
WHICH DESPITEFULLY USE YOU, AND PERSECUTE YOU;

- God has a plan for you, that's all that matters -
  you're about to be promoted!
- He will give you beauty for ashes in the midst of
  your mourning .

JEREMIAH 29:11

11 FOR I KNOW THE THOUGHTS THAT I THINK TOWARD YOU, SAITH
THE LORD, THOUGHTS OF PEACE, AND NOT OF EVIL, TO GIVE YOU AN
EXPECTED END.

ISAIAH 61:3

3 TO APPOINT UNTO THEM THAT MOURN IN ZION, TO GIVE UNTO
THEM BEAUTY FOR ASHES, THE OIL OF JOY FOR MOURNING, THE
GARMENT OF PRAISE FOR THE SPIRIT OF HEAVINESS; THAT THEY MIGHT
BE CALLED TREES OF RIGHTEOUSNESS, THE PLANTING OF THE LORD,
THAT HE MIGHT BE GLORIFIED.

- Jesus dipped the bread and shared it with Judas at the Passover feast - Judas was sitting in the place of honor, and that was an act of favor. So even though Jesus knew what Judas had planned, He showed him honor.

How Jesus responded to the original Judas betrayal:

* Jesus said One of you will betray me in Matthew 26:21.

- Jesus blessed the bread and broke it, and fed the disciples in Matthew 26:26.
- * They sang a hymn together in   Matt 26:30.
- Jesus said All of you will be offended because of Me in Matthew 26:31.
- Jesus continued to serve and wash feet, knowing He was being betrayed. He also spoke to the disciples about humility.

We also are to confirm our love for the person or persons who caused us grief.

6 SUFFICIENT TO SUCH A MAN IS THIS PUNISHMENT, WHICH WAS INFLICTED OF MANY.

7 SO THAT CONTRARIWISE YE OUGHT RATHER TO FORGIVE HIM, AND COMFORT HIM, LEST PERHAPS SUCH A ONE SHOULD BE SWALLOWED UP WITH OVERMUCH SORROW.

8 WHEREFORE I BESEECH YOU THAT YE WOULD CONFIRM YOUR LOVE TOWARD HIM.

9 FOR TO THIS END ALSO DID I WRITE, THAT I MIGHT KNOW THE PROOF OF YOU, WHETHER YE BE OBEDIENT IN ALL THINGS.

10 TO WHOM YE FORGIVE ANY THING, I FORGIVE ALSO: FOR IF I FORGAVE ANY THING, TO WHOM I FORGAVE IT, FOR YOUR SAKES FORGAVE I IT IN THE PERSON OF CHRIST;

11 LEST SATAN SHOULD GET AN ADVANTAGE OF US: FOR WE ARE NOT IGNORANT OF HIS DEVICES. *(EMPHASIS MINE)*

LUKE 22:32

32 BUT I HAVE PRAYED FOR THEE, THAT THY FAITH FAIL NOT: AND WHEN THOU ART CONVERTED, STRENGTHEN THY BRETHREN.

MATTHEW 26:41

41 WATCH AND PRAY, THAT YE ENTER NOT INTO TEMPTATION: THE SPIRIT INDEED IS WILLING, BUT THE FLESH IS WEAK.

- Jesus prayed for the others who were still with Him as He was being betrayed, knowing they would also suffer in Luke 22:32.
- Jesus said Watch and pray that you enter not into temptation - Matthew 26:41.

We need to watch and pray also because we usually don't know beforehand like Jesus did when we are about to be betrayed, and it's easier to get into the flesh when you're blindsided with a huge hurt. He told me some time back to pray every day for Him to remove anyone sent by the enemy to steal, kill or destroy in my life. I added slander to that, and my prayer became:

Lord, I pray you would remove any person from my life who has been sent to steal, kill, destroy or slander me or the ministry in any way whatsoever.

LUKE 22:51

51 AND JESUS ANSWERED AND SAID, SUFFER YE THUS FAR. AND HE TOUCHED HIS EAR, AND HEALED HIM.

- Jesus restored those around Him who were wounded by Judas betrayal where He could - Luke 22:51.
- Jesus knew there was a higher purpose in Judas' betrayal, and He submitted His will to the Father's will Matthew 26:42, that the greater good might come out of the situation, and God be glorified through it.
- Jesus called Judas friend even up to the moment of betrayal - Matthew 26:50.

Matthew 26:42

42 He went away again the second time, and prayed, saying, O my Father, if this cup may not pass away from me, except I drink it, thy will be done.

Matthew 26:50

50 And Jesus said unto him, Friend, wherefore art thou come? Then came they, and laid hands on Jesus and took him.

- Jesus continued to prophesy the future God had promised Him, even as the accusers attacked Him. He never lost sight of His future, or the prize - Matthew 26:64. It is important when experiencing a Judas Test, that you do not lose sight of your promises, either.

Matthew 26:64

64 Jesus saith unto him, Thou hast said: nevertheless I say unto you, Hereafter shall ye see the Son of man sitting on the right hand of power, and coming in the clouds of heaven.

Chapter 13 - The Judas In You

Betrayal is treachery and disloyalty instead of being trustworthy. It is unfaithfulness, and violation of the trust and confidence of someone close . Instead of being a friend and acting in love and protecting, it is becoming an enemy, acting with intent to expose, to take from, to destroy, acting out of spite or revenge. It is someone formerly believed to be loyal who no longer is.

We all want to believe we could never be capable of betraying another the way Judas betrayed Jesus, but is it realistic to think we couldn't? Do we think we are superior to Peter, who walked with Jesus in the flesh, confident we will stand, and only setting ourselves up for a fall? Is there any way to know?

There is a reason Judas asked Jesus who the betrayer was - because everyone has the potential to be a betrayer. Though we may be quick to judge another who betrays, we all betray the Lord any time we sin. If we will betray Him who died a death of great agony for us, we can certainly betray another person, and only our pride keeps us from seeing that we can.

Though normally we are loyal and faithful friends and followers, under other circumstances we might easily find ourselves acting like Judas. Living in the end times, when circumstances can change suddenly and drastically, we would all do well to examine our hearts for how far we might be willing to betray another in order to survive or take care of loved ones.

Imagining end times scenarios is one way to examine what is most important to us.

What if, for example, tomorrow morning you wake up to news reports that all the food and water in the nation where you live has been irreversibly contaminated. All you have is what is in the house with you.

You have a very close friend who is someone who has helped you and your family in the past who has a small storage built up of food, medicine and fresh water, but they need it for themselves and their family.

Weeks go by, you ration your food and water, and still there is no hope in sight of getting more. Even with your best efforts, no more food or water is anywhere to be had at any price, and at last the day comes when you run out.

More weeks pass, and one morning the person you love most in all the world - your parent, grandparent, spouse, child or grandchild - falls ill from lack of food and water. In spite of your best efforts to care for them, you look into their eyes and realize they are slipping away. Within a few days, they will be gone. Your friend has what they need to live and you plead with them, but they refuse to give it up, preferring to keep it for thier own loved ones. You know a way you could get it from them, but it would require you betray them.

What would you do?

As you see your most precious loved one nearing death, would you just sit there and watch them die or would you betray your friend to prevent them dying a horrible death? You choose.

One night in my prayer time during the months when I was writing this book, the Lord spoke to me a message about Judas behavior that He wanted relayed in this book to you, the readers.

I wish for them to see and know how I view such treacherous behavior against My people. Those who return evil for good shall be repaid in kind.

When He spoke that second sentence, I heard very intense anger in His voice.

I wish for My people to know this - that I do not stand by idly as they attack My other children, regardless of their motives. If they cause a brother or sister in the faith harm, I shall repay them.

Many go about wrecking reputations and tearing down ministries in My Holy Name whom I have not sent. If I did not send them, then they were sent by another not of Me. Such treachery shall not go unrepaid. They shall receive in kind to themselves what they have done to others.

Many of My children wonder that I have not promoted them, but how can I when their behavior is thus? They fail to make themselves ready by walking in My ways.

My children are called to preach the gospel, to heal the sick, to minister to the brokenhearted, yet they go about slandering their brethren while My lambs go unfed and the lost wander in darkness.

I found myself wondering later how many people complain to God for not having this or that, or an abundance of provision when they are walking in offense, wrecking the reputations of others, and thereby diminishing that other person's provision. We know we will reap whatever we sow. Sometimes we fail to consider the consequences of our words and actions carefully enough. Sometimes we criticize another out of not only pride but also envy, as Judas did. When we wish bad on them and slander their reputation, we bring those consequences on ourselves.

GALATIANS 6:7

BE NOT DECEIVED; GOD IS NOT MOCKED: FOR WHATSOEVER A MAN SOWETH, THAT SHALL HE ALSO REAP.

2 SAMUEL 12:10

10 NOW THEREFORE THE SWORD SHALL NEVER DEPART FROM THINE HOUSE; BECAUSE THOU HAST DESPISED ME, AND HAST TAKEN THE WIFE OF URIAH THE HITTITE TO BE THY WIFE.

The penalty for returning evil for good is very severe. We can see the effects of this very thing in King David's house, after he conspired and had Uriah killed in battle. The sword never departed from his house after that.

WHOSO REWARDETH EVIL FOR
GOOD, EVIL SHALL NOT DEPART
FROM HIS HOUSE.

- PROVERBS 17:13

Chapter 14 - The End

Ultimately, the Judas Test is about trusting God during some of the most trying seasons of our Christian walks. It is about refusing to let our flesh dictate our responses when someone close to us betrays our trust.

Satan entered Judas and influenced him to betray Jesus. Many accusers accuse because of envy, just as the Pharisees accused Jesus out of envy. I find it very interesting that the Strong's definition of envy in the following verse literally means "ill will." The Pharisees truly did wish Jesus ill - even to the point of death by crucifixion.

MATTHEW 27:17-18

THEREFORE WHEN THEY WERE GATHERED TOGETHER, PILATE SAID UNTO THEM, WHOM WILL YE THAT I RELEASE UNTO YOU? BARABBAS, OR JESUS WHICH IS CALLED CHRIST?

18 FOR HE KNEW THAT FOR ENVY THEY HAD DELIVERED HIM.

When Satan left Judas, he came to his senses and realized what he had done, but he was unable to undo the damage.

MATTHEW 27:3-5

3 THEN JUDAS, WHICH HAD BETRAYED HIM, WHEN HE SAW THAT HE
WAS CONDEMNED, REPENTED HIMSELF, AND BROUGHT AGAIN THE
THIRTY PIECES OF SILVER TO THE CHIEF PRIESTS AND ELDERS,

4 SAYING, I HAVE SINNED IN THAT I HAVE BETRAYED THE INNOCENT
BLOOD. AND THEY SAID, WHAT IS THAT TO US? SEE THOU TO THAT.

5 AND HE CAST DOWN THE PIECES OF SILVER IN THE TEMPLE, AND
DEPARTED, AND WENT AND HANGED HIMSELF.

The price of betrayal is so high! Our God is a God of Justice,
He always avenges His children! Even if another of His
children has attacked you, His justice will prevail.

GALATIANS 6:7 BE NOT DECEIVED; GOD IS NOT MOCKED: FOR
WHATSOEVER A MAN SOWETH, THAT SHALL HE ALSO REAP.

There is no way around reaping what we have sown, so the
person who sows betrayal will likewise reap betrayal. Look
at these Biblical examples:

Sown: David lay with Bathsheba, then had her husband
Uriah killed in war so he could have her.

Reaped: Joab went behind King David's back and had his
son Absalom killed, against his orders.

2 SAMUEL 18:9-15

9 AND ABSALOM MET THE SERVANTS OF DAVID. AND ABSALOM RODE
UPON A MULE, AND THE MULE WENT under the thick BOUGHS OF A
GREAT OAK, AND HIS HEAD CAUGHT HOLD OF THE OAK, AND HE WAS
TAKEN UP BETWEEN THE HEAVEN AND THE EARTH; AND THE MULE THAT
WAS UNDER HIM WENT AWAY.

10 AND A CERTAIN MAN SAW IT, AND TOLD JOAB, AND SAID, BEHOLD, I SAW ABSALOM HANGED IN AN OAK.

11 AND JOAB SAID UNTO THE MAN THAT TOLD HIM, AND, BEHOLD, THOU SAWEST HIM, AND WHY DIDST THOU NOT SMITE HIM THERE TO THE GROUND? AND I WOULD HAVE GIVEN THEE TEN SHEKELS OF SILVER, AND A GIRDLE.

12 AND THE MAN SAID UNTO JOAB, THOUGH I SHOULD RECEIVE A THOUSAND SHEKELS OF SILVER IN MINE HAND, YET WOULD I NOT PUT FORTH MINE HAND AGAINST THE KING'S SON: FOR IN OUR HEARING THE KING CHARGED THEE AND ABISHAI AND ITTAI, SAYING, BEWARE THAT NONE TOUCH THE YOUNG MAN ABSALOM.

13 OTHERWISE I SHOULD HAVE WROUGHT FALSEHOOD AGAINST MINE OWN LIFE: FOR THERE IS NO MATTER HID FROM THE KING, AND THOU THYSELF WOULDEST HAVE SET THYSELF AGAINST ME.

14 THEN SAID JOAB, I MAY NOT TARRY THUS WITH THEE. AND HE TOOK THREE DARTS IN HIS HAND, AND THRUST THEM THROUGH THE HEART OF ABSALOM, WHILE HE WAS YET ALIVE IN THE MIDST OF THE OAK.

15 AND TEN YOUNG MEN THAT BARE JOAB'S ARMOUR COMPASSED ABOUT AND SMOTE ABSALOM, AND SLEW HIM.

Sown: David took Bathsheba, though she was not his wife.

Reaped: Amnon took David's daughter, Tamar, though she was not *his* wife.

2 SAMUEL 13:1-19

13 AND IT CAME TO PASS AFTER THIS, THAT ABSALOM THE SON OF DAVID HAD A FAIR SISTER, WHOSE NAME WAS TAMAR; AND AMNON THE SON OF DAVID LOVED HER.

2 AND AMNON WAS SO VEXED, THAT HE FELL SICK FOR HIS SISTER TAMAR; FOR SHE WAS A VIRGIN; AND AMNON THOUGHT IT HARD FOR HIM TO DO ANYTHING TO HER.

3 BUT AMNON HAD A FRIEND, WHOSE NAME WAS JONADAB, THE SON OF SHIMEAH DAVID'S BROTHER: AND JONADAB WAS A VERY SUBTIL MAN.

4 AND HE SAID UNTO HIM, WHY ART THOU, BEING THE KING'S SON, LEAN FROM DAY TO DAY? WILT THOU NOT TELL ME? AND AMNON SAID UNTO HIM, I LOVE TAMAR, MY BROTHER ABSALOM'S SISTER.

5 AND JONADAB SAID UNTO HIM, LAY THEE DOWN ON THY BED, AND MAKE THYSELF SICK: AND WHEN THY FATHER COMETH TO SEE THEE, SAY UNTO HIM, I PRAY THEE, LET MY SISTER TAMAR COME, AND GIVE ME MEAT, AND DRESS THE MEAT IN MY SIGHT, THAT I MAY SEE IT, AND EAT IT AT HER HAND.

6 SO AMNON LAY DOWN, AND MADE HIMSELF SICK: AND WHEN THE KING WAS COME TO SEE HIM, AMNON SAID UNTO THE KING, I PRAY THEE, LET TAMAR MY SISTER COME, AND MAKE ME A COUPLE OF CAKES IN MY SIGHT, THAT I MAY EAT AT HER HAND.

7 THEN DAVID SENT HOME TO TAMAR, SAYING, GO NOW TO THY BROTHER AMNON'S HOUSE, AND DRESS HIM MEAT.

8 SO TAMAR WENT TO HER BROTHER AMNON'S HOUSE; AND HE WAS LAID DOWN. AND SHE TOOK FLOUR, AND KNEADED IT, AND MADE CAKES IN HIS SIGHT, AND DID BAKE THE CAKES.

9 AND SHE TOOK A PAN, AND POURED THEM OUT BEFORE HIM; BUT HE REFUSED TO EAT. AND AMNON SAID, HAVE OUT ALL MEN FROM ME. AND THEY WENT OUT EVERY MAN FROM HIM.

10 AND AMNON SAID UNTO TAMAR, BRING THE MEAT INTO THE CHAMBER, THAT I MAY EAT OF THINE HAND. AND TAMAR TOOK THE

CAKES WHICH SHE HAD MADE, AND BROUGHT THEM INTO THE CHAMBER TO AMNON HER BROTHER.

11 AND WHEN SHE HAD BROUGHT THEM UNTO HIM TO EAT, HE TOOK HOLD OF HER, AND SAID UNTO HER, COME LIE WITH ME, MY SISTER.

12 AND SHE ANSWERED HIM, NAY, MY BROTHER, DO NOT FORCE ME; FOR NO SUCH THING OUGHT TO BE DONE IN ISRAEL: DO NOT THOU THIS FOLLY.

13 AND I, WHITHER SHALL I CAUSE MY SHAME TO GO? AND AS FOR THEE, THOU SHALT BE AS ONE OF THE FOOLS IN ISRAEL. NOW THEREFORE, I PRAY THEE, SPEAK UNTO THE KING; FOR HE WILL NOT WITHHOLD ME FROM THEE.

14 HOWBEIT HE WOULD NOT HEARKEN UNTO HER VOICE: BUT, BEING STRONGER THAN SHE, FORCED HER, AND LAY WITH HER.

15 THEN AMNON HATED HER EXCEEDINGLY; SO THAT THE HATRED WHEREWITH HE HATED HER WAS GREATER THAN THE LOVE WHEREWITH HE HAD LOVED HER. AND AMNON SAID UNTO HER, ARISE, BE GONE.

16 AND SHE SAID UNTO HIM, THERE IS NO CAUSE: THIS EVIL IN SENDING ME AWAY IS GREATER THAN THE OTHER THAT THOU DIDST UNTO ME. BUT HE WOULD NOT HEARKEN UNTO HER.

17 THEN HE CALLED HIS SERVANT THAT MINISTERED UNTO HIM, AND SAID, PUT NOW THIS WOMAN OUT FROM ME, AND BOLT THE DOOR AFTER HER.

18 AND SHE HAD A GARMENT OF DIVERS COLOURS UPON HER: FOR WITH SUCH ROBES WERE THE KING'S DAUGHTERS THAT WERE VIRGINS APPARELLED. THEN HIS SERVANT BROUGHT HER OUT, AND BOLTED THE DOOR AFTER HER.

19 And Tamar put ashes on her head, and rent her garment of divers colours that was on her, and laid her hand on her head, and went on crying.

Sown: King David had Bathsheba's husband, Uriah, killed to get what he wanted.

Reaped: Absalom had his half brother, Amnon, killed to get what he wanted. Later, Joab also betrays King David, and kills Absalom to get what he wanted.

2 Samuel 13:20-36

20 And Absalom her brother said unto her, Hath Amnon thy brother been with thee? but hold now thy peace, my sister: he is thy brother; regard not this thing. So Tamar remained desolate in her brother Absalom's house.

21 But when king David heard of all these things, he was very wroth.

22 And Absalom spake unto his brother Amnon neither good nor bad: for Absalom hated Amnon, because he had forced his sister Tamar.

23 And it came to pass after two full years, that Absalom had sheepshearers in Baalhazor, which is beside Ephraim: and Absalom invited all the king's sons.

24 And Absalom came to the king, and said, Behold now, thy servant hath sheepshearers; let the king, I beseech thee, and his servants go with thy servant.

25 And the king said to Absalom, Nay, my son, let us not all now go, lest we be chargeable unto thee. And he pressed him: howbeit he would not go, but blessed him.

26 Then said Absalom, If not, I pray thee, let my brother Amnon go with us. And the king said unto him, Why should he go with thee?

27 But Absalom pressed him, that he let Amnon and all the king's sons go with him.

28 Now Absalom had commanded his servants, saying, Mark ye now when Amnon's heart is merry with wine, and when I say unto you, Smite Amnon; then kill him, fear not: have not I commanded you? Be courageous, and be valiant.

29 And the servants of Absalom did unto Amnon as Absalom had commanded. Then all the king's sons arose, and every man gat him up upon his mule, and fled.

30 And it came to pass, while they were in the way, that tidings came to David, saying, Absalom hath slain all the king's sons, and there is not one of them left.

31 Then the king arose, and tare his garments, and lay on the earth; and all his servants stood by with their clothes rent.

32 And Jonadab, the son of Shimeah David's brother, answered and said, Let not my lord suppose that they have slain all the young men the king's sons; for Amnon only is dead: for by the appointment of Absalom this hath been determined from the day that he forced his sister Tamar.

33 Now therefore let not my lord the king take the thing to his heart, to think that all the king's sons are dead: for Amnon only is dead.

34 BUT ABSALOM FLED. AND THE YOUNG MAN THAT KEPT THE WATCH LIFTED UP HIS EYES, AND LOOKED, AND, BEHOLD, THERE CAME MUCH PEOPLE BY THE WAY OF THE HILL SIDE BEHIND HIM.

35 AND JONADAB SAID UNTO THE KING, BEHOLD, THE KING'S SONS COME: AS THY SERVANT SAID, SO IT IS.

36 AND IT CAME TO PASS, AS SOON AS HE HAD MADE AN END OF SPEAKING, THAT, BEHOLD, THE KING'S SONS CAME, AND LIFTED UP THEIR VOICE AND WEPT: AND THE KING ALSO AND ALL HIS SERVANTS WEPT VERY SORE.

Sown: King David betrayed the Lord and His love when he chose to rebel against Him and sin with Bathsheba.

Reaped: Absalom betrayed King David and his love when he chose to rebel, kill Amnon, and try to take the kingdom from him.

2 SAMUEL 18

18 AND DAVID NUMBERED THE PEOPLE THAT WERE WITH HIM, AND SET CAPTAINS OF THOUSANDS, AND CAPTAINS OF HUNDREDS OVER THEM.

2 AND DAVID SENT FORTH A THIRD PART OF THE PEOPLE UNDER THE HAND OF JOAB, AND A THIRD PART UNDER THE HAND OF ABISHAI THE SON OF ZERUIAH, JOAB'S BROTHER, AND A THIRD PART UNDER THE HAND OF ITTAI THE GITTITE. AND THE KING SAID UNTO THE PEOPLE, I WILL SURELY GO FORTH WITH YOU MYSELF ALSO.

3 BUT THE PEOPLE ANSWERED, THOU SHALT NOT GO FORTH: FOR IF WE FLEE AWAY, THEY WILL NOT CARE FOR US; NEITHER IF HALF OF US DIE, WILL THEY CARE FOR US: BUT NOW THOU ART WORTH TEN THOUSAND OF US: THEREFORE NOW IT IS BETTER THAT THOU SUCCOUR US OUT OF THE CITY.

4 AND THE KING SAID UNTO THEM, WHAT SEEMETH YOU BEST I WILL DO. AND THE KING STOOD BY THE GATE SIDE, AND ALL THE PEOPLE CAME OUT BY HUNDREDS AND BY THOUSANDS.

5 AND THE KING COMMANDED JOAB AND ABISHAI AND ITTAI, SAYING, DEAL GENTLY FOR MY SAKE WITH THE YOUNG MAN, EVEN WITH ABSALOM. AND ALL THE PEOPLE HEARD WHEN THE KING GAVE ALL THE CAPTAINS CHARGE CONCERNING ABSALOM.

6 SO THE PEOPLE WENT OUT INTO THE FIELD AGAINST ISRAEL: AND THE BATTLE WAS IN THE WOOD OF EPHRAIM;

7 WHERE THE PEOPLE OF ISRAEL WERE SLAIN BEFORE THE SERVANTS OF DAVID, AND THERE WAS THERE A GREAT SLAUGHTER THAT DAY OF TWENTY THOUSAND MEN.

8 FOR THE BATTLE WAS THERE SCATTERED OVER THE FACE OF ALL THE COUNTRY: AND THE WOOD DEVOURED MORE PEOPLE THAT DAY THAN THE SWORD DEVOURED.

9 AND ABSALOM MET THE SERVANTS OF DAVID. AND ABSALOM RODE UPON A MULE, AND THE MULE WENT UNDER THE THICK BOUGHS OF A GREAT OAK, AND HIS HEAD CAUGHT HOLD OF THE OAK, AND HE WAS TAKEN UP BETWEEN THE HEAVEN AND THE EARTH; AND THE MULE THAT WAS UNDER HIM WENT AWAY.

10 AND A CERTAIN MAN SAW IT, AND TOLD JOAB, AND SAID, BEHOLD, I SAW ABSALOM HANGED IN AN OAK.

11 AND JOAB SAID UNTO THE MAN THAT TOLD HIM, AND, BEHOLD, THOU SAWEST HIM, AND WHY DIDST THOU NOT SMITE HIM THERE TO THE GROUND? AND I WOULD HAVE GIVEN THEE TEN SHEKELS OF SILVER, AND A GIRDLE.

12 AND THE MAN SAID UNTO JOAB, THOUGH I SHOULD RECEIVE A THOUSAND SHEKELS OF SILVER IN MINE HAND, YET WOULD I NOT PUT

FORTH MINE HAND AGAINST THE KING'S SON: FOR IN OUR HEARING THE KING CHARGED THEE AND ABISHAI AND ITTAI, SAYING, BEWARE THAT NONE TOUCH THE YOUNG MAN ABSALOM.

13 OTHERWISE I SHOULD HAVE WROUGHT FALSEHOOD AGAINST MINE OWN LIFE: FOR THERE IS NO MATTER HID FROM THE KING, AND THOU THYSELF WOULDEST HAVE SET THYSELF AGAINST ME.

14 THEN SAID JOAB, I MAY NOT TARRY THUS WITH THEE. AND HE TOOK THREE DARTS IN HIS HAND, AND THRUST THEM THROUGH THE HEART OF ABSALOM, WHILE HE WAS YET ALIVE IN THE MIDST OF THE OAK.

15 AND TEN YOUNG MEN THAT BARE JOAB'S ARMOUR COMPASSED ABOUT AND SMOTE ABSALOM, AND SLEW HIM.

16 AND JOAB BLEW THE TRUMPET, AND THE PEOPLE RETURNED FROM PURSUING AFTER ISRAEL: FOR JOAB HELD BACK THE PEOPLE.

17 AND THEY TOOK ABSALOM, AND CAST HIM INTO A GREAT PIT IN THE WOOD, AND LAID A VERY GREAT HEAP OF STONES UPON HIM: AND ALL ISRAEL FLED EVERY ONE TO HIS TENT.

18 NOW ABSALOM IN HIS LIFETIME HAD TAKEN AND REARED UP FOR HIMSELF A PILLAR, WHICH IS IN THE KING'S DALE: FOR HE SAID, I HAVE NO SON TO KEEP MY NAME IN REMEMBRANCE: AND HE CALLED THE PILLAR AFTER HIS OWN NAME: AND IT IS CALLED UNTO THIS DAY, ABSALOM'S PLACE.

19 THEN SAID AHIMAAZ THE SON OF ZADOK, LET ME NOW RUN, AND BEAR THE KING TIDINGS, HOW THAT THE LORD HATH AVENGED HIM OF HIS ENEMIES.

20 AND JOAB SAID UNTO HIM, THOU SHALT NOT BEAR TIDINGS THIS DAY, BUT THOU SHALT BEAR TIDINGS ANOTHER DAY: BUT THIS DAY THOU SHALT BEAR NO TIDINGS, BECAUSE THE KING'S SON IS DEAD.

21 THEN SAID JOAB TO CUSHI, GO TELL THE KING WHAT THOU HAST SEEN. AND CUSHI BOWED HIMSELF UNTO JOAB, AND RAN.

22 THEN SAID AHIMAAZ THE SON OF ZADOK YET AGAIN TO JOAB, BUT HOWSOEVER, LET ME, I PRAY THEE, ALSO RUN AFTER CUSHI. AND JOAB SAID, WHEREFORE WILT THOU RUN, MY SON, SEEING THAT THOU HAST NO TIDINGS READY?

23 BUT HOWSOEVER, SAID HE, LET ME RUN. AND HE SAID UNTO HIM, RUN. THEN AHIMAAZ RAN BY THE WAY OF THE PLAIN, AND OVERRAN CUSHI.

24 AND DAVID SAT BETWEEN THE TWO GATES: AND THE WATCHMAN WENT UP TO THE ROOF OVER THE GATE UNTO THE WALL, AND LIFTED UP HIS EYES, AND LOOKED, AND BEHOLD A MAN RUNNING ALONE.

25 AND THE WATCHMAN CRIED, AND TOLD THE KING. AND THE KING SAID, IF HE BE ALONE, THERE IS TIDINGS IN HIS MOUTH. AND HE CAME APACE, AND DREW NEAR.

26 AND THE WATCHMAN SAW ANOTHER MAN RUNNING: AND THE WATCHMAN CALLED UNTO THE PORTER, AND SAID, BEHOLD ANOTHER MAN RUNNING ALONE. AND THE KING SAID, HE ALSO BRINGETH TIDINGS.

27 AND THE WATCHMAN SAID, ME THINKETH THE RUNNING OF THE FOREMOST IS LIKE THE RUNNING OF AHIMAAZ THE SON OF ZADOK. AND THE KING SAID, HE IS A GOOD MAN, AND COMETH WITH GOOD TIDINGS.

28 AND AHIMAAZ CALLED, AND SAID UNTO THE KING, ALL IS WELL. AND HE FELL DOWN TO THE EARTH UPON HIS FACE BEFORE THE KING, AND SAID, BLESSED BE THE LORD THY GOD, WHICH HATH DELIVERED UP THE MEN THAT LIFTED UP THEIR HAND AGAINST MY LORD THE KING.

29 AND THE KING SAID, IS THE YOUNG MAN ABSALOM SAFE? AND AHIMAAZ ANSWERED, WHEN JOAB SENT THE KING'S SERVANT, AND ME THY SERVANT, I SAW A GREAT TUMULT, BUT I KNEW NOT WHAT IT WAS.

30 AND THE KING SAID UNTO HIM, TURN ASIDE, AND STAND HERE. AND HE TURNED ASIDE, AND STOOD STILL.

31 AND, BEHOLD, CUSHI CAME; AND CUSHI SAID, TIDINGS, MY LORD THE KING: FOR THE LORD HATH AVENGED THEE THIS DAY OF ALL THEM THAT ROSE UP AGAINST THEE.

32 AND THE KING SAID UNTO CUSHI, IS THE YOUNG MAN ABSALOM SAFE? AND CUSHI ANSWERED, THE ENEMIES OF MY LORD THE KING, AND ALL THAT RISE AGAINST THEE TO DO THEE HURT, BE AS THAT YOUNG MAN IS.

33 AND THE KING WAS MUCH MOVED, AND WENT UP TO THE CHAMBER OVER THE GATE, AND WEPT: AND AS HE WENT, THUS HE SAID, O MY SON ABSALOM, MY SON, MY SON ABSALOM! WOULD GOD I HAD DIED FOR THEE, O ABSALOM, MY SON, MY SON!

If you hold back and don't get into strife or let pride make you start answering back, your Judas Test will work to your good. You will be strengthening your spirit and starving your flesh.

Those who set God's people up for betrayal are orchestrating their own destruction, because Judas always hangs himself in the end.

If you do not pass the Judas Test, take heart - God will let you take it again. He's patient like that.

The good news is, if the Judas Test shows up, it means you are very near the fulfillment of a big promise, for the purpose of the Judas Test is refining your love walk and crucifying your flesh so that God can promote you!

Chapter 15 – Do's and Don'ts for Passing The Judas Test

We are ALL capable of betrayal.

Don't get into disappointment:

PSALM 22:5 (NASB)

5 TO YOU THEY CRIED OUT AND WERE DELIVERED; IN YOU THEY TRUSTED AND WERE NOT DISAPPOINTED.

- Don't judge them. Concentrate on loving and forgiving them instead.
- Don't lift the sword of your mouth to cut them back.
- Don't let the root of bitterness spring up in you.
- Don't open the door to strife by striking back.
- Don't speak death or you will eat the fruits of it
- If the person is communicating with you (for example, by sending emails) and it's making things worse, DON'T READ THEM. Let a friend read them for you, or just ignore them. If your email offends you, turn it off. A lot of fights could be avoided if we ignored some people's emails and Facebook.

- When you *do* communicate with the Judas person who hurt you, communicate as if everyone you know, including your boss, your Pastor AND Jesus, were going to hear every word of your communication, because that could actually happen when you are communicating with an enemy.
- Learn to recognize when you've been hit with a fiery dart and pull them out right away. Pull the darts out, place your hand on your stomach (or wherever you feel the pain) and say, I plead the precious Blood of Jesus over those word wounds and I declare them destroyed, in Jesus' mighty Name!
- Avoid the temptation to gossip, to tell everyone you know how badly you've been wronged, and how horrible your betrayer is. That is biting and devouring another, or gnashing your teeth on them.

GALATIANS 5:15

15 BUT IF YE BITE AND DEVOUR ONE ANOTHER, TAKE HEED THAT YE BE NOT CONSUMED ONE OF ANOTHER.

If you gossip, or slander their character, you are planting seeds that will bring up a mighty harvest in your own life.

* Do not use requesting prayer as an excuse to tell everyone what they did to you, either! That is the same thing as gossiping, and if you gossip or slander, you fail the test and lose your promotion. Using prayer requests as a way to tell your story under the guise of something besides gossip or slander is just slapping a Christian label over your sin and no one is fooled, including the person you request the prayer from.

When we hurt, we want to tell people, and this is a very difficult part of passing the test, but if you never stop talking about when someone hurt you, did you know you will never forgive them? We don't want to leave this earth with unforgivenes, or we will be turned over to the tormentors.

- Remind yourself often that your goal is to PASS the test!
- If you pass the test, a strong anointing from it will rest on your life, but only if you do it God's way.
- Do praise - including FOR the betrayal - this opens the door for God to bless you in it
- DO thank God for everything about the situation, even if you have to do it through gritted teeth and in your squeaky voice
- DO worship – worshipping when you are hurting is the most powerful worship of all!
- Encourage yourself and your faith by remembering other times when God helped you.
- *DO increase your time in His presence and don't spend that time complaining! Pour your pain out at His feet. He is very near to the brokenhearted. Let His love wrap around you like a warm blanket and take comfort there.
- Fight against feeling offended, angry, bitter and resentful. These will hinder you in passing the test. Remember: God sees everything that happened, and He *always* defends His children!
- Pray for God's will to be done, or pray the Lord's prayer. I like to pray Psalm 23 during these times as well.
- Don't stop bearing fruit for the Kingdom
- Increase your prayer time and your time in God's Word. And don't forget to pray for your enemies.
- Don't allow what happened to you to take away your ability to trust.
- Remember at all times that your emotions are likely going to be your biggest enemy and Satan will

control them if you don't. This is the worst possible time to do anything based on your "feelings," so make sure you are led by God's Spirit and not your emotions.

- Strive to walk in love, humility and forgiveness. If you can do this, you will be promoted, and they will be demoted after the test is over.
- Don't get frustrated if you can't hear God right now. Remember, the teacher is always silent during the test!
- Playing praise and worship music will help you keep your peace and stay focused.
- Guard your heart and your thoughts at all times. Don't let the enemy have free rent in your head by putting bad thoughts in there.

Study how Jesus responded.

- Jesus gave them the one new commandment to love one another, right after Judas left to betray him (John 13:34)
- Communion: Remember His sacrifice
- He washed the feet of the Disciples - SERVE OTHERS
- Jesus prayed for Peter, that his faith would not fail (Luke 22)
- Jesus said "If you love Me, keep My commandments" - John 14:15
- Jesus continued to call Judas friend, even knowing he was anything but - this might have been a last ditch effort to bring repentance to Judas' heart, or may have been Jesus loving others as He always did

PR∩Y – SERVE – LOVE.

- Peter, James and John slept during the betrayal (Matt. 26:40, Mk 14:37) Jesus told them they should be praying. (Luke 22:46, Mk 14:38)
- Don't join the crowd and go with swords and staves to help crucify the accused. (Matt 26:47)
- Don't attack another servant of God (one of Jesus' followers cut off the ear of Malchus, a servant of the High Priest - John 18:10)
- Don't lie against the accused or mock them if you witness another's Judas Test. Minister to them instead.
- Don't distance yourself from someone you know is innocent out of fear of association. (Peter followed from afar - Matt. 26:58, Lk 22:54)

More From Glynda

Glynda Lomax is also the author of the "Curse Breaking Series," a series of eBooks available in Kindle version from Amazon.com on how to break generational, sin and word curses off your life.

These eBooks and all their print books are also available through her website, www.wingsofprophecy.com.

Print books also available at www.amazon.com.

Wings of Prophecy – From the Beginning

What is God saying to His people, to the Church in America, and to this nation as a whole? How close are we to the end of this Age as we know it, and what events will tell us when we are in it? What special instructions and observations does God have for those who want to be included in the Bride of Jesus Christ? Where does the Rapture fit into all of this? These questions and many more will be addressed in Wings of Prophecy - From the Beginning.

The Wilderness Companion

A road map through the desert experiences in your life.

Every Christian must pass through the desert on the way to their Promised Land. Wilderness experiences are often times of great uncertainty and change. Our time in the desert seasons of our lives is lengthened or shortened depending on our response to each circumstance. Our faith in Christ is refined in the intense heat of the desert experience as our intimacy with Him increases. Find out how to go from surviving to thriving by partnering with God as He leads you in the path that will strengthen your faith and prepare you to step into your destiny. The Wilderness Companion will help you.

The Healing Companion

A road map to your healing! Have you struggled with the promises of healing in the Holy Bible, not understanding why you could not make them yours? Have you, like me, tried reading, listening, confessing, and everything else you can think of, only to fall back into sickness again? Would you like to learn the truth about Biblical healing, once and for all, in a way that is understandable and easy to apply to your own life? Walk with me through my healing journeys and learn what God taught me about healing as I struggled to understand, and came out healed from every effect of a hemorrhagic stroke that nearly killed me. Learn the steps to healing, and why they MUST be done in order. Learn why you confess over and over that you are healed and you still do not see the manifestation.

If this book has been a blessing to you, I would love to hear from you! You can contact me at:

wingsofprophecy@gmail.com   or by mail at:

Glynda Lomax

P.O. Box 127

Princeton, TX 75407

NOTES

NOTES:

66503946R00060

Made in the USA
Lexington, KY
15 August 2017